HOW TO HAVE A LIFE

ANCIENT WISDOM FOR MODERN READERS

■ ■ ■ ■

For a full list of titles in the series, go to https://press
.princeton.edu/series/ancient-wisdom-for-modern-readers.

HOW TO HAVE
A LIFE

■ ■ ■ ■ ■

An Ancient Guide to Using Our Time Wisely

Seneca

Selected, translated, and introduced
by James S. Romm

PRINCETON UNIVERSITY PRESS
PRINCETON AND OXFORD

Published by Princeton University Press
41 William Street, Princeton, New Jersey 08540
99 Banbury Road, Oxford OX2 6JX

press.princeton.edu

All Rights Reserved

ISBN 9780691219127
ISBN (e-book) 9780691219462

British Library Cataloging-in-Publication Data is available

Editorial: Rob Tempio and Chloe Coy
Production Editorial: Mark Bellis
Text Design: Pamela Schnitter
Jacket Design: Heather Hansen
Production: Erin Suydam
Publicity: Maria Whelan and Carmen Jimenez

Jacket Credit: *Nero and Seneca* © Photographic Archive Museo Nacional del Prado. Sundial, Inv. 51358 © History of Science Museum, University of Oxford.

This book has been composed in Stempel Garamond and Futura

Printed on acid-free paper. ∞

Printed in the United States of America

1 3 5 7 9 10 8 6 4 2

CONTENTS

INTRODUCTION

"No one on his deathbed ever said, I wish I'd spent more time on my business." That oft quoted sentence has been around for about forty years. It was first used by a friend of Massachusetts senator Paul Tsongas, after the senator learned he had cancer. The thought helped convince Tsongas not to run for reelection, as he had planned; he withdrew from politics briefly but returned after successful medical treatment and ran for the Democratic presidential nomination in 1992.

"Life's too short," we often say, in a briefer version of the Tsongas sentence—by which we mean, "I refuse to spend my time,

since that will one day come to an end, on this tedious task." We also speak of "bucket lists," things we hope to do before death arrives, or conduct a thought experiment: "If you had only one day to live . . ." In various ways we try to grasp that time is a finite resource. We also berate ourselves for wasting time and thus deride the internet as a "time suck" or allow our smartphones to remind us of how much time we've spent in the labyrinths they provide (an average of 3.5 hours a day for adults, according to a 2019 study).

Seneca the Younger, who like Paul Tsongas served in the Senate and tried—unsuccessfully—to withdraw from politics, would have approved of the notion that life must be viewed from an imagined deathbed. Indeed, in the essay translated in this book, *De Brevitate Vitae*, or "On the Shortness

of Life," Seneca constantly adopts that perspective. He imagines himself speaking to centenarians, on the brink of the grave, and asking them to total up the days spent on pedestrian tasks, on meeting the needs of others, or on idle, transitory pleasures. When you look at what's left, he advises those in extreme old age, you'll see that you're actually dying *young*.

If Seneca's message were merely "life's too short," his essay might be worth reading, but in fact it goes much farther. Time, it turns out, is *not* the limited resource we think it is. Like money, to which Seneca often compares it, time can be stretched by putting it to good use. We speak of "quality time," but time well used actually has greater *quantity*. A life that extends twenty calendar years might thus be longer than one that attains triple digits. In his most fervent

passages, Seneca even proposes that the best use of time might grant us a kind of immortality. He offers mere hints, at first, at what that best use consists of, then fully explicates it as his essay reaches its climax (I won't spoil the impact of "the big reveal" by anticipating it here).

Along the way to this climax, Seneca lampoons various forms of time wastage, hitting especially hard at business pursuits and gain-seeking. He comes back again and again to the system the Romans called *clientela*, in which poorer "clients," or dependents, went to the homes of wealthy patrons, usually in the early morning, to pay their respects and seek favors or advice. Both patrons and clients, in Seneca's view, are demeaned by this system and made to expend huge amounts of their precious time. Yet Seneca, as we know, took

part in the system himself—a problem we shall return to below.

Little better than those who squander time on business are those so engrossed in a hobby or avocation that they, too, surrender their time to feed their obsession. Under this heading, Seneca castigates those who give lavish dinner parties, who meticulously groom their hair, or who conduct research into obscure historical questions (this last attack sends a chill down the classicist's spine!). All such people are lumped together by Seneca, along with those driven by business and legal pursuits, under the Latin term *occupati*, rendered here (inadequately) as "preoccupied." One by one, Seneca turns his withering glance on each of these *occupati*, such that his treatise becomes, for long stretches, an entertaining piece of social satire.

Wealth and luxury are frequently lurking behind the pursuits of the *occupati*, so Seneca's attacks on wastage of time are also, indirectly, hits at Roman materialism. His ultimate target is the pampered aristocrat who gets carried around from bath to sedan chair by teams of household slaves. This grotesque fellow is so unaware of his surroundings that he can't even tell his own posture; "Am I seated now?" he asks his porters, after they place him in his chair. "How can *he* be the master of any portion of time?" asks Seneca, bringing his diatribe back to its main theme. Great wealth takes us out of ourselves and away from what's real and true; it prevents us from being "masters of time," an intriguing phrase found only here.

Though Seneca writes dismissively about wealth and about the preoccupations of

Rome's elite, it must be noted that he belonged to that elite and was enormously wealthy. Moreover, in the terms of the Roman clientela system, Seneca was an immensely powerful and sought-after patron. At the time "On the Shortness of Life" was written, he was in fact serving as chief minister to young Nero, the ruler of Rome, a post in which Seneca was besieged by clients daily. This paradox raises the problems, faced often by readers of Seneca, of how the man's life measured up to his own ideals and of how to interpret advice that he seems, at first glance anyway, to have himself ignored.

Seneca studied with Stoic teachers in youth, followers of the Greek creed that exalted a life of reason and virtuous action and warned against the dangerous influence of the passions. His talent for expressing

these ideas in hard-hitting prose emerged early on, but so did his interest in Roman politics. He entered the Senate sometime in the AD 30s and made a name for himself there as an orator and speechwriter. He survived (barely) the purges during the reign of Caligula, but then under Claudius, in AD 41, found himself exiled to the island of Corsica. After eight years in the wilderness, he was recalled to Rome to serve as tutor and moral guide to the young Nero, then being groomed as Claudius's likely successor.

When Nero became emperor at age seventeen, in AD 54, Seneca's presence at court became a valued political asset. Agrippina, Nero's controlling mother, gave Seneca huge authority over her son and thus over the empire. But Nero and his mother soon quarreled, putting Seneca in a difficult position.

Perhaps as the result of one such quarrel, and Agrippina's anger in its aftermath, Seneca's father-in-law, Pompeius Paulinus, was dismissed from his position as *praefectus annonae*, the official in charge of maintaining and distributing Rome's voluminous grain imports. Seneca himself was too valuable to dismiss.

It's noteworthy that "On the Shortness of Life" is addressed to this same Paulinus and deals very directly with his situation, urging him, in its final chapters, to withdraw from management of grain stocks. Perhaps, as scholar Miriam Griffin plausibly argued, Seneca wrote the essay in part to spare his kinsman a public embarrassment, by couching his firing as a happy retirement. If that thesis is accepted, we can date the essay, fairly precisely, to AD 55, the first year of Nero's reign. In any case that date is clearly

the latest point at which it could have been written, since Paulinus is said to be still in charge of the grain.

By AD 55 Seneca had only glimpsed the troubles he was to endure as a man of reason and moderation who had joined a tempestuous court. In the decade to come, he would be forced to collude, actively or passively, in dynastic murders, including that of Agrippina, and abet some of Nero's strange passions. He had his hands full meanwhile with oversight of the empire, a circumstance at odds with his advice in this essay. When he writes "That man who has gained the longed-for rods wants to set them aside, and immediately wonders 'When will my term be over?'" he might well be talking about himself. He never had the "rods," the *fasces* that symbolized high authority, carried before him as other high officials did, but he

bore just as heavy a burden as they, if not heavier.

While serving as Nero's de facto chief of staff, Seneca also grew rich, far richer than most in his day—another problem for his modern readers. As mentioned above, in "On the Shortness of Life," Seneca often speaks of gain-getting as the source of much of our wastage of time and lampoons pampered rich men and powerful patrons. No doubt he conducted his own patronage— his daily reception of favor- and influence- seekers—in a manner different from the callous scorn he depicts here, and he claims (in other writings) to have had a healthy indifference toward his own wealth. But he was attacked in his own day for profiteering even while preaching the meaninglessness of money, and those attacks have continued ever since. It's hard to avoid the conclusion

that he wanted to have things two ways, or (more charitably) that he set a higher standard for others than he lived up to himself.

From where he stood in AD 55 or a few years before, Seneca could not have foreseen the difficulties he would endure as a member of Nero's court. Had he known what lay ahead, as Nero descended into bizarre, delusional behavior and committed dynastic murders, Seneca would surely have tried to get out of the palace, but by the time he *did* try—around AD 62—it was too late; Nero needed his presence too badly, as a prop to his regime's sagging image. The three years that followed, the last of Seneca's life, were spent in a strange kind of limbo; though still a high court official, Seneca tried his best to stay out of the limelight and out of Nero's destructive path. In these years he

composed his philosophical magnum opus, the *Moral Epistles*, two excerpts from which are included in this volume to show that Seneca continued to ponder the problem of time even as he sensed his own time running out.

The end came in AD 65, when Nero uncovered a plot on his life that involved many of Seneca's friends and the poet Lucan, Seneca's nephew. Seneca may or may not have been part of the plot, but Nero, according to Tacitus, had long been seeking a pretext to destroy his former teacher, who was by now an irksome reminder of his better self. He had Seneca's villa surrounded by soldiers and ordered Seneca to commit suicide, a common means in imperial Rome of doing away with political enemies. Seneca met his death, again according to Tacitus,

with courage and equipoise, even when the task of killing himself became protracted and painful.

In his own day, Seneca was highly regarded as a prose stylist (and perhaps as a poet as well, though we have far less evidence of how his verse tragedies were received). His treatises crackle with passionate intensity, mordant humor, and compelling exempla, all expressed in a streamlined, hard-hitting prose all Seneca's own. In the present volume, I have tried to convey the feel of that prose, even at the risk of producing an unnatural-sounding English. I have tried to let Seneca speak in his own voice, though I've pluralized some of his pronouns to avoid the overwhelming male bias of the original Latin.

The message of "On the Shortness of Life" overlaps with that of the Tsongas sentence,

in that Seneca urges us to view life from the deathbed and not to take our time on earth for granted, since it is inevitably brief. But the essay also goes far beyond a mere exhortation to spend less time at the office. It calls on us to truly *live*, as Seneca defines true life—a definition many readers will find surprising and unfamiliar. If the essay causes them to rethink what "life" means and to reconsider their use of time, Seneca will have accomplished his goal.

DE BREVITATE VITAE

I. Maior pars mortalium, Pauline, de naturae malignitate conqueritur, quod in exiguum aevi gignimur, quod haec tam velociter, tam rapide dati nobis temporis spatia decurrant, adeo ut exceptis admodum paucis ceteros in ipso vitae apparatu vita destituat. Nec huic publico, ut opinantur, malo turba tantum et imprudens vulgus ingemuit; clarorum quoque virorum hic affectus querellas evocavit. Inde illa maximi medicorum exclamatio est: "vitam brevem esse, longam artem." Inde Aristotelis cum rerum natura exigentis minime conveniens

ON THE SHORTNESS OF LIFE

[1] Most of humankind, Paulinus,[1] complains about the spitefulness of Nature, on grounds that we're born for a short life span and that these moments of time that have been given to us dart away so quickly, so swiftly, that only a few escape this pattern: life deserts us when we're just getting ready for life. It's not only the crowd and the thoughtless mob that's grieved by this universal ill (as they think it to be); it draws, as well, the impassioned laments of leaders. Hence, one hears that well-known saying of the greatest of doctors:[2] "Life is short, but art is long." Or the complaint, so unbefitting a philosopher, voiced by Aristotle as he quarreled with

sapienti viro lis: "aetatis illam animalibus tantum indulsisse, ut quina aut dena saecula educerent, homini in tam multa ac magna genito tanto citeriorem terminum stare." Non exiguum temporis habemus, sed multum perdidimus. Satis longa vita et in maximarum rerum consummationem large data est, si tota bene collocaretur; sed ubi per luxum ac neglegentiam diffluit, ubi nulli bonae rei impenditur, ultima demum necessitate cogente, quam ire non intelleximus transisse sentimus. Ita est: non accipimus brevem vitam sed fecimus, nec inopes eius sed prodigi sumus. Sicut amplae et regiae opes, ubi ad malum dominum pervenerunt, momento dissipantur, at quamvis modicae, si bono custodi traditae sunt, usu crescunt:

Nature: "She lavished so much life span on the animals that they can stretch out their existence for five or ten ages, but set such a quicker endpoint for humankind, a race born for so many great endeavors."[3]

In fact, our time is not short, but we squander much of it. Life's long enough and generously allotted to allow us to achieve great things, if it were well spent; but when it seeps away through pleasure-seeking and lack of awareness, when it is dispensed for no good thing, then, as the final necessity bears down, we realize that the life we didn't feel passing has already gone past. It's like this: life's not short when we get it, but we *make* it so; we're not poor in life but wasteful of it. Just as plentiful and princely wealth can be scattered in a moment if it comes to a wicked master, while it grows when deployed by a good caretaker, so our life span

ita aetas nostra bene disponenti multum patet.

II. Quid de rerum natura querimur? Illa se benigne gessit: vita, si uti scias, longa est. Alium insatiabilis tenet avaritia; alium in supervacuis laboribus operosa sedulitas; alius vino madet, alius inertia torpet; alium defetigat ex alienis iudiciis suspensa semper ambitio, alium mercandi praeceps cupiditas circa omnis terras, omnia maria spe lucri ducit; quosdam torquet cupido militiae numquam non aut alienis periculis intentos aut suis anxios; sunt quos ingratus superiorum cultus voluntaria servitute consumat; multos aut affectatio alienae formae aut suae querella detinuit; plerosque nihil certum sequentis vaga et inconstans et sibi displicens levitas per nova consilia iactavit; quibusdam nihil quo cursum derigant

has ample extent for those who manage it well.

[2] Why do we complain about Nature? She's full of kindness. Life is long if you know how to make use of it. But insatiable greed holds some in its grip; a toilsome devotion to useless endeavors, others; this one is sodden with wine, that one grows sluggish with idleness; ambition, always dependent on outside opinions, exhausts this one, while that one is led through all lands and seas by restless zeal for trade and hope of profit. Some are tormented by a desire for soldiering, always intent on injuries to others or worried over those to themselves; some are made slaves, of their own will, through unrequited attendance on higher-ups. Then there's the crowd that pursues no fixed goal—their restless, shifting, discontented shallowness tosses them about from

placet, sed marcentis oscitantisque fata deprendunt, adeo ut quod apud maximum poetarum more oraculi dictum est verum esse non dubitem: "Exigua pars est vitae qua vivimus." Ceterum quidem omne spatium non vita sed tempus est. Urgent et circumstant vitia undique nec resurgere aut in dispectum veri attollere oculos sinunt. Et immersos et in cupiditatem infixos premunt, numquam illis recurrere ad se licet. Si quando aliqua fortuito quies contigit, velut profundo mari, in quo post ventum quoque volutatio est, fluctuantur nec umquam illis a cupiditatibus suis otium stat. De istis me putas dicere, quorum in confesso mala sunt? Aspice illos ad quorum felicitatem concurritur:bonis suis effocantur. Quam

one plan to the next—and others who aren't content with *any* goal they might have pursued, who meet their end slouching and yawning, confirming for me that what the greatest of poets has said, in the manner of an oracle, is true: "It's only a sliver of life that we actually *live*."[4] All the rest of the span is not life but only time.

Vices surround and oppress us everywhere. They prevent us from lifting our eyes for a view of the truth, but rather push them downward and keep them fixed on our desires. People are never allowed to return to their true selves. If a chance space of calm comes upon them, they're like the deep sea, which rolls with swells after a gale; they are still rolled about and never find any release from their desires. Do you think I'm speaking of *those*, who have undeniable faults? Just look at *these*, whose good

multis divitiae graves sunt! Quam multo-
rum eloquentia et cotidiana ostentandi in-
genii sollicitatio sanguinem educit! Quam
multi continuis voluptatibus pallent! Quam
multis nihil liberi relinquit circumfusus clientium populus! Omnis denique istos ab
infimis usque ad summos pererra: hic advo-
cat, hic adest, ille periclitatur, ille defendit,
ille iudicat, nemo se sibi vindicat, alius in
alium consumitur. Interroga de istis quorum nomina ediscuntur, his illos dinosci
videbis notis: ille illius cultor est, hic illius;

fortune draws others in throngs;[5] they're suffocated by their own successes. How many have found wealth a burden! How many have had their blood drained on account of their eloquence and their obsession with showing off talent each and every day! How many grow pale through constant pursuit of pleasure! How many have no freedom left, when a crowd of dependents surrounds them? Look them over, all of them, from those at the bottom right up to the top. One hires a lawyer, another takes the case, a third stands at the dock, a fourth mounts the defense, a fifth acts as judge, yet none of them sue to reclaim *themselves*; each one is used up for another's sake.

Go ahead and ask about those whose names are on everyone's lips. You'll see how they differ one from another: The first plays up to the second, the second to the third;

suus nemo est. Deinde dementissima quorundam indignatio est: queruntur de superiorum fastidio, quod ipsis adire volentibus
non vacaverint! Audet quisquam de alterius
superbia queri, qui sibi ipse numquam vacat?
Ille tamen te, quisquis es, insolenti quidem
vultu sed aliquando respexit, ille aures suas
ad tua verba demisit, ille te ad latus suum
recepit: tu non inspicere te umquam, non
audire dignatus es. Non est itaque quod ista
officia cuiquam imputes, quoniam quidem,
cum illa faceres, non esse cum alio volebas,
sed tecum esse non poteras.

III. Omnia licet quae umquam ingenia fulse-
runt in hoc unum consentiant, numquam

none belong to themselves. Then think of
the outrage, insane though it is, of those
who complain about the arrogance of higher-
ups, saying they don't make time for those
who desire a meeting. Does anyone dare
to complain about the arrogance of another,
while never making time for him- or herself? Here's one who deigns to notice you
(whoever you are) now and then, though
with haughty expression; who opens his
ears to your words and who admits you
to his presence; yet you didn't think it
worth your while to look at or hear *yourself*. You've got no right to expect anyone
to pay you back for those services; when
you offered them, it was not from a wish to
be with someone else but an inability to be
with yourself.

[3] Though all the bright spirits that ever
blazed concur on this point, still they can

satis hanc humanarum mentium caliginem mirabuntur: praedia sua occupari a nullo patiuntur et, si exigua contentio est de modo finium, ad lapides et arma discurrunt; in vitam suam incedere alios sinunt, immo vero ipsi etiam possessores eius futuros inducunt; nemo invenitur qui pecuniam suam dividere velit, vitam unusquisque quam multis distribuit! Adstricti sunt in continendo patrimonio, simul ad iacturam temporis ventum est, profusissimi in eo cuius unius honesta avaritia est. Libet itaque ex seniorum turba comprendere aliquem: "Pervenisse te ad ultimum aetatis humanae videmus, centesimus tibi vel supra premitur annus: agedum, ad computationem aetatem tuam revoca. Duc

never be astonished enough at the fog that besets human minds. No one lets their property get seized; if even a tiny dispute arises over boundaries, people dash for stones and weapons. Yet they allow others to invade their very life, or indeed they themselves install those who will carve off swaths of its territory. You'll find no one who voluntarily shares his money, yet to how many do we each give shares of our life! People are stingy when it comes to conserving estates, but the moment it comes to expenditure of *time*, the one thing for which it's honorable to be greedy, they're spendthrifts.

Let's get hold of someone out of the multitude of the elderly and say: "We see that you've arrived at that final stage of human life; you're bearing down on your hundredth year or more. Come then, summon

quantum ex isto tempore creditor, quantum amica, quantum rex, quantum cliens abstulerit, quantum lis uxoria, quantum servorum coercitio, quantum officiosa per urbem discursatio; adice morbos quos manu fecimus, adice quod et sine usu iacuit: videbis te pauciores annos habere quam numeras. Repete memoria tecum quando certus consilii fueris, quotus quisque dies ut destinaveras recesserit, quando tibi usus tui fuerit, quando in statu suo vultus, quando animus intrepidus, quid tibi in tam longo aevo facti operis sit, quam multi vitam tuam diripuerint te non sentiente quid perderes, quantum vanus dolor, stulta laetitia, avida cupiditas,

your life span for an accounting. Reckon up how much of that time a creditor, mistress, ruler, or client stole away; how much an argument with your wife or the scolding of your slaves, how much your dashing about town on needful tasks; then add the illnesses we bring on ourselves, add the time spent doing nothing; you'll see that your number of years does not measure up to your original count.

"Search back in your memory for the time when your resolve was firm—how few days ended up as you'd planned!—when you had full control of yourself; when your face wore its natural expression; when your mind felt no fear. Think of what you can claim to have done in so long a life; how many people have taken chunks of your life while you didn't notice what you were losing; how much was lost to empty grief, to

blanda conversatio abstulerit, quam exiguum tibi de tuo relictum sit: intelleges te immaturum mori." Quid ergo est in causa? Tamquam semper victuri vivitis, numquam vobis fragilitas vestra succurrit, non obseruatis quantum iam temporis transierit; velut ex pleno et abundanti perditis, cum interim fortasse ille ipse qui alicui vel homini vel rei donatur dies ultimus sit. Omnia tamquam mortales timetis, omnia tamquam immortales concupiscitis. Audies plerosque dicentes: "A quinquagesimo anno in otium secedam, sexagesimus me annus ab officiis dimittet." Et quem tandem longioris vitae praedem accipis? Quis ista sicut disponis ire patietur? Non pudet te reliquias vitae tibi reservare et id

foolish elation, to greedy desire, to fawning socializing; how little a part of your time you still own; then you'll understand that you're in fact dying too soon."

How to explain it? You live as though you'll be alive forever, not taking account of your human fragility; you don't notice how much time has gone by; you squander it as though from a full and heaping store, while that very day that's spent on some person or thing might be your last one. Your fears about all things are those of mortals; your desires of all things, those of immortals. One hears a lot of people saying, "I'll cut back and take things easy when I'm fifty, and my sixtieth year will release me from duties." And what guarantee of a longer life have you gotten? Who will permit those things to proceed as you've planned them? Aren't you ashamed to set aside the

solum tempus bonae menti destinare quod
in nullam rem conferri possit? Quam serum
est tunc vivere incipere cum desinendum est!
Quae tam stulta mortalitatis oblivio in quin-
quagesimum et sexagesimum annum differre
sana consilia et inde velle vitam inchoare quo
pauci perduxerunt!

IV. Potentissimis et in altum sublatis hominibus excidere voces videbis quibus otium
optent, laudent, omnibus bonis suis praefer-
ant. Cupiunt interim ex illo fastigio suo, si
tuto liceat, descendere; nam ut nihil extra
lacessat aut quatiat, in se ipsa fortuna ruit.
Diuus Augustus, cui dii plura quam ulli

remnants of life for yourself and devote to higher thought only that portion of time that can't be put to any business matter? How late to begin to live, at the point that life must be left behind! How foolish to ignore mortality and put off sound pursuits[6] to one's fiftieth or sixtieth year and to want to start life at a point to which few have attained!

[4] You'll notice that even the most powerful people, those who've ascended to the heights, drop hints about the repose they long for, praise, or place above all other priorities. They often want to climb down from that high ledge they're on, if it can be done safely; for even though no external force disturbs or shakes it, Fortune collapses upon itself, by itself.

The deified Augustus,[7] to whom the gods gave more than to anyone else, never stopped

praestiterunt, non desiit quietem sibi precari et vacationem a re publica petere; omnis eius sermo ad hoc semper revolutus est, ut speraret otium: hoc labores suos, etiam si falso, dulci tamen oblectabat solacio, aliquando se victurum sibi. In quadam ad senatum missa epistula, cum requiem suam non vacuam fore dignitatis nec a priore gloria discrepantem pollicitus esset, haec verba inveni: "Sed ista fieri speciosius quam promitti possunt. Me tamen cupido temporis optatissimi mihi provexit, ut quoniam rerum laetitia moratur adhuc, praeciperem aliquid voluptatis ex verborum dulcedine." Tanta visa est res otium, ut illam, quia usu non poterat, cogitatione praesumeret. Qui

praying for rest and seeking a respite from public affairs. All his conversations kept coming back to his desire for rest; it was by this consolation, sweet even if false—the thought that he'd someday live for himself— that he relieved his toils. I have found the following words in a certain letter he sent to the Senate,[8] claiming that a respite would not be without dignity nor in conflict with the glory he'd accrued up to that point: "But these matters are more impressive in the execution than the prospect. In any case my desire for that time I most hope for[9] has reached the point that since the joy of attaining the thing itself is still lagging, I'm seeking to get some advance enjoyment from the sweetness of words." That's how great a thing leisure seemed, so great that one who could not yet obtain its use could get a taste of it in his thoughts. The man

omnia videbat ex se uno pendentia, qui hominibus gentibusque fortunam dabat, illum diem laetissimus cogitabat quo magnitudinem suam exueret. Expertus erat quantum illa bona per omnis terras fulgentia sudoris exprimerent, quantum occultarum sollicitudinum tegerent: cum civibus primum, deinde cum collegis, novissime cum affinibus coactus armis decernere mari terraque sanguinem fudit. Per Macedoniam, Siciliam, Aegyptum, Syriam Asiamque et omnis prope oras bello circumactus Romana caede lassos exercitus ad externa bella convertit. Dum Alpes pacat immixtosque mediae paci et imperio hostes perdomat,

who saw everything relying on his sole person, who saw to the success of individuals and nations, regarded with greatest delight that day on which he might set aside his own greatness. He had learned how much sweat was wrung from him by those blessings that shone out on every land, how many hidden worries they concealed. He'd been forced to wage war first with fellow citizens, then with his colleagues, and finally with in-laws;[10] he'd spilled blood by land and by sea. Compelled to march through Macedonia, Sicily, Egypt, Syria, Asia Minor, and nearly every coast, he unleashed the armed forces, weary of Roman slaughter, on foreign wars. While he was subduing the Alps and enemies nestled in amid the empire and at peace, while he was pushing our boundaries past the Danube and Rhine and Euphrates, here in Rome

dum ultra Rhenum et Euphraten et Danu-
vium terminos movet, in ipsa urbe Mure-
nae, Caepionis Lepidi, Egnati, aliorum
in eum mucrones acuebantur. Nondum
horum effugerat insidias: filia et tot nobiles
iuvenes adulterio velut sacramento adacti
iam infractam aetatem territabant Iullusque
et iterum timenda cum Antonio mulier.
Haec ulcera cum ipsis membris absciderat:
alia subnascebantur; velut grave multo san-
guine corpus parte semper aliqua rumpe-
batur. Itaque otium optabat, in huius spe
et cogitatione labores eius residebant, hoc
votum erat eius qui voti compotes facere
poterat.

V. M. Cicero inter Catilinas, Clodios iactatus
Pompeiosque et Crassos, partim manifestos

itself, the blades of Murena, Caepio, Lepidus, Egnatius, and others were whetted against him.[11] And he was not yet free of those conspiracies when his daughter and so many highborn youths, confederate in adultery as though in a sacred vow, brought constant alarm to his now broken years, along with Iullus and yet another woman who, when paired with an Antony, had to be feared.[12] As soon as he'd excised these sores by cutting off his very limbs, others opened up in their place; just as in a body sodden with too much blood, there was always a hemorrhage in one place or another. And so he longed for a peaceful disengagement; his toils found relief in the hope and contemplation of this. This was the wish of one who could make others' wishes come true.

[5] Marcus Cicero, beset by Catilines and Clodiuses, Pompeys and Crassuses—some,

inimicos, partim dubios amicos, dum fluc-
tuatur cum re publica et illam pessum eun-
tem tenet, novissime abductus, nec secundis
rebus quietus nec adversarum patiens, quo-
tiens illum ipsum consulatum suum non
sine causa sed sine fine laudatum detestatur!
Quam flebiles voces exprimit in quadam ad
Atticum epistula iam victo patre Pompeio,
adhuc filio in Hispania fracta arma refo-
vente! "Quid agam," inquit, "hic, quaeris?
Moror in Tusculano meo semiliber." Alia
deinceps adicit, quibus et priorem aetatem
complorat et de praesenti queritur et de futura desperat. Semiliberum se dixit Cicero: at
me hercules numquam sapiens in tam hu-
mile nomen procedet, numquam semiliber
erit, integrae semper libertatis et solidae,

open enemies; others, treacherous friends—
while being tossed on rough seas along
with the republic, and keeping the state
from going under, was at last swept away.[13]
He was neither at peace in good times nor
able to bear up when things went against
him. How often did he curse that very consulship that he'd once praised (not without
cause but without cease)! How many woe-
ful expressions he used in a certain letter to
Atticus, when Pompey the father was already beaten but Pompey the son was still
reviving his broken strength in Spain.[14]
"What am I to do here, you ask?" he writes.
"I'm detained on my Tusculan estate, half-
free." He adds other thoughts, lamenting his
earlier life, complaining about his present
one, despairing of the one to come. Cicero
called himself "half-free;" but I swear, a sage
will never aspire to such a lowly term, and

solutus et sui iuris et altior ceteris. Quid enim supra eum potest esse qui supra fortunam est?

VI. Livius Drusus, vir acer et vehemens, cum leges novas et mala Gracchana movisset stipatus ingenti totius Italiae coetu, exitum rerum non pervidens, quas nec agere licebat nec iam liberum erat semel incohatas relinquere, exsecratus inquietam a primordiis vitam dicitur dixisse: uni sibi ne puero quidem umquam ferias contigisse. Ausus est enim et pupillus adhuc et praetextatus iudicibus reos commendare et gratiam suam foro interponere tam efficaciter quidem, ut quaedam iudicia constet ab illo

indeed will never be "half-free," but will always be free in a whole and pure sense, unconstrained, master of himself, higher than everything else.

[6] Livius Drusus[15] was a keen and industrious man. Once, when he had moved radical legislation and stirred up the ills of the days of the Gracchi,[16] with a huge throng from all of Italy surrounding him, seeing no good end for the undertakings that could neither be brought to fulfillment nor abandoned once set in motion, calling down curses on a life that had been busy from its outset, he is said to have said, "I alone have never seen a day of rest, even in childhood." When still a young lad, not yet in an adult's toga, he had the courage to plead for defendants in front of judges and exert influence in the courts, so effectively that he beat the odds by winning some verdicts. Such a

rapta. Quo non erumperet tam immatura ambitio? Scires in malum ingens et privatum et publicum evasuram praecoquem audaciam. Sero itaque querebatur nullas sibi ferias contigisse a puero seditiosus et foro gravis. Disputatur an ipse sibi manus attulerit; subito enim vulnere per inguen accepto collapsus est, aliquo dubitante an mors eius voluntaria esset, nullo an tempestiva. Supervacuum est commemorare plures qui, cum aliis felicissimi viderentur, ipsi in se verum testimonium dixerunt perosi omnem actum annorum suorum; sed his querellis nec alios mutaverunt nec se ipsos: nam cum verba

precocious ambition might have burst forth in any direction. But you might have known that immature boldness such as his would result in great injury, both personal and public. Too late did he complain that he'd never seen a day off, since from boyhood he was combative and troublesome to the Forum. There's debate over whether he took his own life. He collapsed all of a sudden after receiving a wound that entered through the groin; some doubted whether his death was self-willed, but none that it was timely.

It's pointless to evoke more instances of those who, though seemingly happier than others, gave evidence against themselves showing that they despised every action they took in their lives. With their complaints, moreover, they changed neither others nor themselves, for after words have

eruperunt, affectus ad consuetudinem relabuntur. Vestra me hercules vita, licet supra mille annos exeat, in artissimum contrahetur: ista vitia nullum non saeculum devorabunt; hoc vero spatium, quod quamvis natura currit ratio dilatat, cito vos effugiat necesse est; non enim apprenditis nec retinetis vel ocissimae omnium rei moram facitis, sed abire ut rem supervacuam ac reparabilem sinitis.

VII. In primis autem et illos numero qui nulli rei nisi vino ac libidini vacant; nulli enim turpius occupati sunt. Ceteri, etiam si vana gloriae imagine teneantur, speciose

spilled out, feelings slide back into old patterns.

Really, the life that you all live,[17] even if it lasts over a thousand years, will shrink into a tiny space. Those vices you practice will consume every century. Truly that space of time that Reason prolongs, even though it's naturally prone to rush past, must flee from you with all speed. You fail to grab it and hold it back or put delays in the path of the fastest thing of all, but you let it go by as though it were worthless or easy to replenish.

[7] First among these I count those who make time for nothing except drink and sex; there's no one more shamefully occupied than they. Then there are those who are gripped by a vain mirage of glory (though these people go astray in a seemly fashion); then you can add the greedy, the wrathful,

tamen errant; licet avaros mihi, licet iracun-
dos enumeres vel odia exercentes iniusta vel
bella, omnes isti virilius peccant: in ventrem
ac libidinem proiectorum inhonesta tabes
est. Omnia istorum tempora excute, aspice quam diu computent, quam diu insi-
dientur, quam diu timeant, quam diu colant,
quam diu colantur, quantum vadimonia sua
atque aliena occupent, quantum convivia,
quae iam ipsa officia sunt: videbis quemadmodum illos respirare non sinant vel mala
sua vel bona. Denique inter omnes convenit
nullam rem bene exerceri posse ab homine
occupato, non eloquentiam, non liberales
disciplinas, quando districtus animus nihil

and those who engage in unjust hatreds or wars (all these are more vigorous sinners; the stain on those who give themselves up to their lust or their belly is a shameful one).[18] Examine the way that each of these groups spend their time: how long they count up their gains, think up plots, or cower in fear; how long they fawn or are fawned on; how long they dwell on their own courtroom dates or those of the ones they are suing; how long they spend at dinner parties, when these, too, have turned into business occasions. Take all in all and you'll see how they give no breathing room to their own doings, whether good ones or bad ones.

In sum, it's agreed by all that no subject can be well pursued by those whose attention is elsewhere, neither oratory nor the liberal arts, for the mind that's pulled every

altius recipit sed omnia velut inculcata respuit. Nihil minus est hominis occupati quam vivere: nullius rei difficilior scientia est. Professores aliarum artium vulgo multique sunt, quasdam vero ex his pueri admodum ita percepisse visi sunt, ut etiam praecipere possent: vivere tota vita discendum est et, quod magis fortasse miraberis, tota vita discendum est mori. Tot maximi viri, relictis omnibus impedimentis, cum divitiis, officiis, voluptatibus renuntiassent, hoc unum in extremam usque aetatem egerunt ut vivere scirent; plures tamen ex his nondum se scire confessi vita abierunt, nedum ut isti

which way takes in nothing very deeply but rejects all things as though they were forced upon it. Nothing belongs less to the distracted person than living;[19] no subject is harder to understand. There are teachers of other arts, many and easy to find; indeed, some arts even boys seem to take in well enough to teach others. But living must be learned through a whole lifetime, and— you'll perhaps marvel at this even more— dying, too, must be learned through a whole lifetime. So many of the greatest men, when all obstacles have fallen away, when they have renounced wealth, duties, and pleasures, have pursued this one goal into extreme old age, to learn how to live, yet most have departed life admitting they don't yet know how; still less do those others less great!

sciant. Magni, mihi crede, et supra humanos errores eminentis viri est nihil ex suo
tempore delibari sinere, et ideo eius vita
longissima est, quia, quantumcumque pa-
tuit, totum ipsi vacavit. Nihil inde incul-
tum otiosumque iacuit, nihil sub alio fuit,
neque enim quicquam repperit dignum
quod cum tempore suo permutaret custos
eius parcissimus. Itaque satis illi fuit: iis vero
necesse est defuisse ex quorum vita multum
populus tulit. Nec est quod putes illos
non aliquando intellegere damnum suum:
plerosque certe audies ex iis quos magna
felicitas gravat inter clientium greges aut
causarum actiones aut ceteras honestas mise-
rias exclamare interdum: "Vivere mihi non
licet." Quidni non liceat? Omnes illi qui te

Trust me: it's the mark of great people, and of those who tower over human fallibility, to let no portion of time slip away; it's they who have the longest lives, since whatever portion is free is entirely available for their use. Nothing lay idle or fallow, nothing was commandeered by another; the most scrupulous stewards of time find nothing that's worth giving their time in exchange for. That's why time suffices for them, whereas for others, from whose life the public takes away much time, it must always be lacking. And there's no reason to think they don't sometimes understand the curse that's upon them. You'll hear many of those weighed down by great prosperity call out, from amid their flocks of dependents,[20] their legal maneuvers, and their other "respectable" torments, "I'm not permitted to *live*!" Obviously you're not! Because all

sibi advocant tibi abducunt. Ille reus quot dies abstulit? Quot ille candidatus? Quot illa anus efferendis heredibus lassa? Quot ille ad irritandam avaritiam captantium simulatus aeger? Quot ille potentior amicus, qui vos non in amicitiam sed in apparatu habet? Dispunge, inquam, et recense vitae tuae dies: videbis paucos admodum et reiculos apud te resedisse. Assecutus ille quos optaverat fasces cupit ponere et subinde dicit: "Quando hic annus praeteribit?" Facit ille ludos, quorum sortem sibi obtingere magno aestimavit: "Quando," inquit, "istos effugiam?" Diripitur ille toto foro patronus et magno concursu omnia ultra quam audiri

those who call you to come to their aid take you away from yourself. How many days did that defendant steal? Or that candidate for office? Or that old woman, worn out from burying heirs?[21] Or that pretend invalid, stirring up the greed of the legacy hunters? Or that high and mighty "friend," whose purpose is not to be your friend but to put you on show? Tick off and count up the days of your life: you'll see that few, and useless ones, were entirely in your possession.

That man who has gained the longed-for rods[22] wants to set them aside and immediately asks "When will my term be over?" Another puts on games, a job he reckoned was worth a fortune to get, but says: "When will I be rid of them?" And a third, a legal defender, is lionized by the whole Forum and packs the whole place with a crowd, so

potest complet: "Quando," inquit, "res pro-
ferentur?" Praecipitat quisque vitam suam
et futuri desiderio laborat, praesentium tae-
dio. At ille qui nullum non tempus in usus
suos confert, qui omnes dies tamquam vitam
ordinat, nec optat crastinum nec timet. Quid
enim est quod iam ulla hora novae voluptatis possit afferre? Omnia nota, omnia ad
satietatem percepta sunt. De cetero fors
fortuna ut volet ordinet: vita iam in tuto
est. Huic adici potest, detrahi nihil, et adici
sic quemadmodum saturo iam ac pleno
aliquid cibi: quod nec desiderat et capit.

greatly that he can't be heard: "When," he says, "will I get a vacation?" All of us hasten our lives along, in toil over yearning for the future and disappointment with the present.

But the people who don't amass any time except for their own purposes, who arrange each day as though it contained a whole life, neither long for tomorrow nor dread it. For what new kind of pleasure can any passing hour add to our store? Everything is already known; everything has been enjoyed to the full. Let Fortune arrange the future however she will; life is already secured. It can be added to but not diminished in any way, and added to in the same way as a morsel of food for a person who's sated and full and doesn't want more but still makes room for it.

Non est itaque quod quemquam propter canos aut rugas putes diu vixisse: non ille diu vixit, sed diu fuit. Quid enim, si illum multum putes navigasse quem saeva tempestas a portu exceptum huc et illuc tulit ac vicibus ventorum ex diverso furentium per eadem spatia in orbem egit? Non ille multum navigavit, sed multum iactatus est.

VIII. Mirari soleo cum video aliquos tempus petentes et eos qui rogantur facillimos; illud uterque spectat propter quod tempus petitum est, ipsum quidem neuter: quasi nihil petitur, quasi nihil datur. Re omnium pretiosissima luditur; fallit autem illos, quia res incorporalis est, quia sub oculos non venit

There's no reason to think someone's lived long on account of their gray hair and wrinkles. That person only existed, not lived, a long time. Would you say that a man has done much voyaging, if, as soon as he left port, a violent storm seized him and, with furious blasts of wind arising from every direction, drove him in a circle over and over the same route? He didn't do much journeying; he was only much tossed around.

[8] I often marvel at those who request the time of others and at those who grant those requests obligingly. Both groups look to the reason the time was wanted; neither looks to the time itself. It's as though nothing had been sought and nothing given. People play games with the most valuable thing of all. They're deceived because it's a thing without substance, a thing not seen

ideoque vilissima aestimatur, immo paene nullum eius pretium est. Annua, congiaria homines carissime accipiunt et illis aut laborem aut operam aut diligentiam suam locant: nemo aestimat tempus; utuntur illo laxius quasi gratuito. At eosdem videbis, si mortis periculum propius admotum est, medicorum genua tangentes, si metuunt capitale supplicium, omnia sua, ut vivant, paratos impendere! Tanta in illis discordia affectuum est! Quodsi posset quemadmodum praeteritorum annorum cuiusque numerus proponi, sic futurorum, quomodo illi qui paucos viderent superesse trepidarent, quomodo illis parcerent! Atqui facile est quamvis exiguum dispensare quod

with the eyes; they think it's the cheapest of commodities, indeed that it has practically no worth at all. People put a high value on getting salaries and handouts, and devote their effort, their labor, their zeal to these things; but no one values time; they spend it lavishly, as though it were free. You'll see those same people, if the threat of death comes near, taking the knees of their doctors in supplication, or if they fear the death penalty, making ready to swap all their goods for the right to live. That's how inconstant their emotions are. But if for each person the number of years to come could be set forth just like the number of years gone by, how they'd tremble if they saw they had only a few left, and how they'd hoard them! But in fact it's easy to manage a small amount of a thing, if you're sure of the quantity; it's the thing that you don't

certum est; id debet servari diligentius quod nescias quando deficiat. Nec est tamen quod putes illos ignorare quam cara res sit: dicere solent eis quos valdissime diligunt paratos se partem annorum suorum dare: dant nec intellegunt: dant autem ita ut sine illorum incremento sibi detrahant. Sed hoc ipsum an detrahant nesciunt; ideo tolerabilis est illis iactura detrimenti latentis. Nemo restituet annos, nemo iterum te tibi reddet. Ibit qua coepit aetas nec cursum suum aut revocabit aut supprimet; nihil tumultuabitur, nihil admonebit velocitatis suae: tacita labetur. Non illa se regis imperio, non favore populi

know how long it will last that ought to be more carefully conserved.

There's no reason to think that *those* people are unaware of how precious time is, for they often say to the ones for whom they deeply care that they're ready to give them a part of their own years. They give it, alright, without realizing; but they give it in such a way that they take away from themselves without adding to the portion of others. Indeed, they don't even know whether or not they take it away from themselves, and thus they put up with the loss of what they don't notice losing.

No one will restore the years; no one will return you to yourself. Life will go forward on the path it began on and won't repeat or halt its course. It won't kick up any fuss or raise alarm at its own swiftness. It will slip away in silence. The power of kings

longius proferet: sicut missa est a primo die, curret, nusquam devertetur, nusquam remorabitur. Quid fiet? Tu occupatus es, vita festinat; mors interim aderit, cui velis nolis vacandum est.

IX. Potestne quicquam esse levius hominum eorum iudicio qui prudentiam iactant? Operosius occupati sunt. Vt melius possint vivere, impendio vitae vitam instruunt. Cogitationes suas in longum ordinant; maxima porro vitae iactura dilatio est: illa primum quemque extrahit diem, illa eripit praesentia dum ulteriora promittit. Maximum vivendi impedimentum est exspectatio, quae pendet ex crastino, perdit hodiernum.

or the acclaim of the masses won't stretch it out longer. It will run on just as it was launched on your first day and will never be turned aside or delayed. How will things turn out? While you keep busy, life hastens on; and all the while death will be there, and you'll have to free up time for *that*, like it or not.

[9] What could be more foolish than the attitude of those who boast of their foresight? They're burdened and busy in an effort to live better; they adorn life by paying out life.[23] They form their thoughts with a long view in mind, but postponement is the greatest waste of a life: it strips away each day in its turn and steals what's before us while promising what's ahead. Anticipation is the greatest obstacle to living; it depends on tomorrow while squandering today.[24] You make neat rows of things that

Quod in manu fortunae positum est disponis, quod in tua, dimittis. Quo spectas?
Quo te extendis? Omnia quae ventura sunt
in incerto iacent: protinus vive. Clamat ecce
maximus vates et velut divino horrore in-
stinctus salutare carmen canit:

> Optima quaeque dies miseris mortalibus
>   aevi
> Prima fugit.

"Quid cunctaris?" inquit, "Quid cessas?
Nisi occupas, fugit." Et cum occupaveris,
tamen fugiet: itaque cum celeritate temporis utendi velocitate certandum est et velut
ex torrenti rapido nec semper ituro cito hau-
riendum. Hoc quoque pulcherrime ad exprobrandam infinitam cogitationem quod

are in Fortune's hands while letting drop what's in your own. What are you looking toward? What are you aiming for? Everything that's to come is cloaked in uncertainty. Live right now!

Listen! The greatest of poets, as though inspired with divine speech, sings a song that can bring us to health:

> Every best day in the life of wretched
> mortals
> is the first day that flees.[25]

"Why do you delay?" he says. "Why do you fail to act? If you don't grab hold, it gets away." And when you *have* grabbed hold, it will flee nonetheless. You must rival the swiftness of time with the speed with which you use it and grab a quick drink as if from a rushing stream that won't always flow.

non optimam quamque aetatem sed diem
dicit. Quid securus et in tanta temporum
fuga lentus menses tibi et annos in longam
seriem, utcumque aviditati tuae visum est,
exporrigis? De die tecum loquitur et de hoc
ipso fugiente. Num dubium est ergo quin
prima quaeque optima dies fugiat mortalibus miseris, id est occupatis? Quorum pu-
erilis adhuc animos senectus opprimit, ad
quam imparati inermesque perveniunt; nihil
enim provisum est: subito in illam necopi-
nantes inciderunt, accedere eam cotidie non
sentiebant. Quemadmodum aut sermo aut
lectio aut aliqua intentior cogitatio iter faci-
entis decipit et pervenisse ante sciunt quam
appropinquasse, sic hoc iter vitae assiduum

And the poet very nicely reproaches endless procrastination when he says "every best day," not "every best lifetime." Why do you, complacent and passive amid so much loss of time, set forth months and years for yourself stretching out into a long row, just as your greediness deems fitting? The poet is telling you about the day that is fleeing before our eyes. For there's no doubt, is there, that "every best day flees" for "wretched mortals"—which is to say, *busy* mortals. Old age, a state they arrive at unprepared and unprotected, bears down on their still-childish minds. Before they know it, they've tumbled into it, for they didn't perceive it creeping up day by day. Just as when a conversation, or a passage from a book, or a very intense thought, distracts those on a journey and they realize they've arrived before they knew they were close—in just

et citatissimum quod vigilantes dormien-
tesque eodem gradu facimus occupatis non
apparet nisi in fine.

X. Quod proposui si in partes velim et argumenta diducere, multa mihi occurrent per
quae probem brevissimam esse occupatorum vitam. Solebat dicere Fabianus, non ex
his cathedrariis philosophis, sed ex veris et
antiquis, "contra affectus impetu, non subtilitate pugnandum, nec minutis vulneribus
sed incursu avertendam aciem." Non pro-
babat cavillationes: "vitia enim contundi
debere, non vellicari." Tamen, ut illis er-
ror exprobretur suus, docendi non tantum

this way, the journey through life, so un-swerving and swift, which we make at the same pace whether awake or asleep, only becomes apparent at its end, for those too busy to notice.

[10] If I should choose to divide my pro-posed topic into parts and separate discus-sions, I'd find many ways to demonstrate that the life of those who are preoccupied is extremely short. Fabianus, who was not from today's schoolroom thinkers but the ancient and true ones,[26] used to say that the fight against the passions must be made by an onrush, not by fine reasoning, and that the foe's battle line must be turned by a frontal assault, not by pinpricks. He didn't approve of quibbling; he said that vices ought to be smashed to bits, not merely pecked at. Still, if the misguided thought of these people is ever to get its comeuppance,

deplorandi sunt. In tria tempora vita dividitur: quod fuit, quod est, quod futurum est. Ex his quod agimus breve est, quod acturi sumus dubium, quod egimus certum. Hoc est enim in quod fortuna ius perdidit, quod in nullius arbitrium reduci potest. Hoc amittunt occupati; nec enim illis vacat praeterita respicere, et si vacet iniucunda est paenitendae rei recordatio. Inviti itaque ad tempora male exacta animum revocant nec audent ea retemptare quorum vitia, etiam quae aliquo praesentis voluptatis lenocinio surripiebantur, retractando patescunt. Nemo, nisi quoi omnia acta sunt sub censura sua,

they'll have to be *taught*, not given up for lost souls.

Our life divides into three time frames: what has been, what is, and what's to come. Of these three, the part we're now living is short, the part we *will* live is uncertain, the part we've already lived is fixed; that's the part that Fortune has no control over, that can't be put under anyone's jurisdiction. But it's this part that's lost in the case of the preoccupied, for they have no time to look back on the past, and even if they do, they get no pleasure from recalling things they regret. They call to mind only unwillingly the time they misused and don't venture to probe again a span whose vices, even those that stole in through some enticement of momentary pleasure, stand revealed by recollection. Only those whose every action was monitored by their own judgment—a

quae numquam fallitur, libenter se in praet-
eritum retorquet: ille qui multa ambitiose
concupiit superbe contempsit, impotenter
vicit insidiose decepit, avare rapuit prodige
effudit, necesse est memoriam suam timeat.
Atqui haec est pars temporis nostri sacra
ac dedicata, omnis humanos casus super-
gressa, extra regnum fortunae subducta,
quam non inopia, non metus, non morbo-
rum incursus exagitet; haec nec turbari nec
eripi potest; perpetua eius et intrepida pos-
sessio est. Singuli tantum dies, et hi per
momenta, praesentes sunt; at praeteriti temporis omnes, cum iusseritis, aderunt, ad

faculty never deceived—turn back willingly toward the past. Those who ambitiously sought much gain, who haughtily showed scorn, who triumphed without restraint, who treacherously deceived, who greedily stole, who recklessly squandered—*they*'re the ones who must fear their own memory. And yet that's the portion of time that's holy and consecrate, beyond the bounds of the chances of human life, severed from the realm that Fortune rules; it can't be disrupted by poverty, fear, or the onsets of diseases; it can't be disturbed or stolen away; it's forever and securely in our grasp. Our days come before us only one at a time, and each one only moment by moment, whereas the days of the past will *all* be there whenever you bid them; they'll allow you to hold onto them and look them over at your

arbitrium tuum inspici se ac detineri patientur, quod facere occupatis non vacat. Securae et quietae mentis est in omnes vitae suae partes discurrere; occupatorum animi, velut sub iugo sint, flectere se ac respicere non possunt. Abit igitur vita eorum in profundum; et ut nihil prodest, licet quantumlibet ingeras, si non subest quod excipiat ac servet, sic nihil refert quantum temporis detur, si non est ubi subsidat: per quassos foratosque animos transmittitur. Praesens tempus brevissimum est, adeo quidem ut quibusdam nullum videatur; in cursu enim semper est, fluit et praecipitatur; ante desinit esse quam venit, nec magis moram patitur quam mundus aut sidera, quorum irrequieta semper agitatio numquam in eodem

discretion—a thing that busy people have no time for.

It's the mark of a peaceful and stable mind to roam through all portions of life. But the minds of the preoccupied are like oxen beneath a yoke; they can't turn about and look backward. Thus, their life disappears into an abyss, and just as you achieve nothing, no matter how much you put in, if there's nothing underneath to catch it and keep it, so in the same way, it doesn't matter how much time is provided; if there's no place for it to settle, it passes right through minds that are porous with cracks and holes.

The present time is so very brief that it seems to some like nothing at all. It's always in motion, flowing and rushing ahead; it has already ceased to exist before it's arrived, and it doesn't suffer delay, any more than the cosmos or planets and stars, whose restless

vestigio manet. Solum igitur ad occupatos praesens pertinet tempus, quod tam breve est ut arripi non possit, et id ipsum illis districtis in multa subducitur.

XI. Denique vis scire quam non diu vivant? Vide quam cupiant diu vivere. Decrepiti senes paucorum annorum accessionem votis mendicant: minores natu se ipsos esse fingunt; mendacio sibi blandiuntur et tam libenter se fallunt quam si una fata decipiant. Iam vero cum illos aliqua imbecillitas mortalitatis admonuit, quemadmodum paventes moriuntur, non tamquam exeant de vita sed tamquam extrahantur. Stultos se fuisse ut non vixerint clamitant et, si modo evaserint ex illa valetudine, in otio victuros;

agitation never stays in one place. That's why *only* present time matters to the preoccupied: it's so brief that it can't be seized hold of, and it's the very thing stolen from *them*, while they're pulled in so many directions.

[11] In sum, do you want to know how short their life is? Look at how long a life they *want*. Ailing old men offer prayers to beg for a few years' extension; they pretend that they're younger than they really are; they flatter themselves by the lie and deceive themselves as eagerly as though they were tricking the fates at the same time. Then when some downturn reminds them of their mortal condition, how fearfully they die, not so much leaving life behind as being dragged out of it. They cry that they've been fools for not having truly *lived* and that if only they escape the current illness, they'll

tunc quam frustra paraverint quibus non fruerentur, quam in cassum omnis ceciderit labor cogitant. At quibus vita procul ab omni negotio agitur, quidni spatiosa sit? Nihil ex illa delegatur, nihil alio atque alio spargitur, nihil inde fortunae traditur, nihil neglegentia interit, nihil largitione detrahitur, nihil supervacuum est: tota, ut ita dicam, in reditu est. Quantulacumque itaque abunde sufficit, et ideo, quandoque ultimus dies venerit, non cunctabitur sapiens ire ad mortem certo gradu.

XII. Quaeris fortasse quos occupatos vocem? Non est quod me solos putes dicere

live henceforth free from duties. They consider how uselessly they prepared for things they would never enjoy, how in vain all their effort has been.

But how can it be that life is not ample for those who've spent it far from every duty? No part of it is consigned to another, no part is scattered here and there, no part is placed in Fortune's power; no part is wasted through neglect or recklessly squandered or left empty; everything's put to work generating return.[27] Thus, however short life may be, it is fully enough. That's why when the last day arrives, the wise will not hesitate to go toward death with a confident step.

[12] Perhaps you ask whom it is I call "preoccupied." You shouldn't suppose I mean only those who are finally chased out of the courts when the guard dogs are let loose,[28] whom you see crushed in their own

quos a basilica immissi demum canes eici-
unt, quos aut in sua vides turba speciosius
elidi aut in aliena contemptius, quos officia
domibus suis evocant ut alienis foribus illi-
dant, hasta praetoris infami lucro et quandoque suppuraturo exercet. Quorundam
otium occupatum est: in villa aut in lecto suo,
in media solitudine, quamvis ab omnibus
recesserint, sibi ipsi molesti sunt: quorum
non otiosa vita dicenda est sed desidiosa
occupatio. Illum tu otiosum vocas qui
Corinthia, paucorum furore pretiosa, anxia
subtilitate concinnat et maiorem dierum
partem in aeruginosis lamellis consumit?

crowd for the sake of show or in another's out of contempt;[29] whose client duties summon them out of their own homes and hurl them against the doorways of others; whom the praetors' spear[30] stirs up, with the hope of a gain that's disreputable and therefore likely to fester.

There are also certain people whose very leisure is preoccupied. In their country homes or their beds, in the midst of solitude, even though they've withdrawn from all cares, they still trouble *themselves*; their life must be termed not one of leisure but rather an idle way of keeping busy. Do you call "relaxed" that person who arranges with anxious precision Corinthian bronzes, their prices bid up by the mania of the elites, and uses up most of the day on rusty metal pots? Or the one who sits beside the wrestling ring, an eager spectator of brawling

qui in ceromate (nam, pro facinus! ne Romanis quidem vitiis laboramus!) spectator
puerorum rixantium sedet? qui iumento-
rum suorum greges in aetatum et colorum
paria diducit ? qui athletas novissimos pas-
cit? Quid? Illos otiosos vocas quibus apud
tonsorem multae horae transmittuntur, dum
decerpitur si quid proxima nocte succrevit,
dum de singulis capillis in consilium itur,
dum aut disiecta coma restituitur aut defi-
ciens hinc atque illinc in frontem compelli-
tur? Quomodo irascuntur, si tonsor paulo
neglegentior fuit, tamquam virum tonderet!
Quomodo excandescunt si quid ex iuba sua
decisum est, si quid extra ordinem iacuit,
nisi omnia in anulos suos reciderunt! Quis

boys (For shame! The vices we struggle against are not even Roman!).[31] Or who segregates troops of his oiled-up athletes[32] by age and skin color, and recruits the freshest young talents?

How's that? Do you say that people are "at leisure" if they let slip countless hours at the hairdresser, while any new growth from the previous night is trimmed away, while counsels are held about individual hairs, while any disarray is restored to its place and thin wisps are combed from both sides to cover a bald pate? How angry they get if the barber gets a tiny bit careless, as if he were grooming a *real* man! How fiery their temper if anything's clipped from their proud mane, if anything's out of position, if it all doesn't cascade into its proper ringlets. Who among these people would not prefer the *republic* to be disturbed rather than

est istorum qui non malit rem publicam turbari quam comam suam? qui non sollicitior
sit de capitis sui decore quam de salute? qui
non comptior esse malit quam honestior?
Hos tu otiosos vocas inter pectinem specu-
lumque occupatos? Quid illi qui componen-
dis, audiendis, discendis canticis operati
sunt, dum vocem, cuius rectum cursum natura et optimum et simplicissimum fecit, in
flexus modulationis inertissimae torquent,
quorum digiti aliquod intra se carmen
metientes semper sonant, quorum, cum ad
res serias, etiam saepe tristes adhibiti sunt,
exauditur tacita modulatio? Non habent
isti otium, sed iners negotium. Convivia

their hair? Which of them would not be more concerned with the beauty of his head than keeping it on his shoulders? Which would choose greater honor over greater style? Do you say that people are "at leisure" if they're obsessed with brushes and mirrors?

How about those preoccupied by composing or listening to songs, or teaching others to sing them? Who twist the human voice, which Nature gave a level register that's plainest and best, into strange turns of the most worthless crooning? Whose fingers are always tapping time along with some song in their heads? Whose quiet singing can be overheard even when they've been directed toward serious, even grave, matters? They have not leisure but rather an idle busyness.

me hercules horum non posuerim inter va-
cantia tempora, cum videam quam solliciti
argentum ordinent, quam diligenter exole-
torum suorum tunicas succingant, quam
suspensi sint quomodo aper a coco exeat,
qua celeritate signo dato glabri ad ministe-
ria discurrant, quanta arte scindantur aves
in frusta non enormia, quam curiose infeli-
ces pueruli ebriorum sputa detergeant: ex
his elegantiae lautitiaeque fama captatur et
usque eo in omnes vitae secessus mala sua
illos sequuntur, ut nec bibant sine ambitione
nec edant. Ne illos quidem inter otiosos nu-
meraveris qui sella se et lectica huc et illuc

And I wouldn't list among leisurely pastimes the dinner parties of *these* people,[33] when I see how anxiously they arrange the silverware, how carefully they tie up the tunics of the boy toys[34] who'll serve the meal, how they wait and watch to see how well the cook dealt with the roast boar, how quickly their smooth-cheeked slaves[35] run to their duties as soon as the trumpet sounds, how skillfully the fowl are carved into delicate portions, how carefully the wretched slave boys wipe up what the drunks have spit out. By these means they get the renown of elegance and refinement. Their vices penetrate so deep into all the quiet corners of their lives that they can't even eat or drink without ostentation.

Nor would I list among those with leisure the people who get around to this place or that by litter or sedan chair, who show up

ferunt et ad gestationum suarum, quasi deserere illas non liceat, horas occurrunt, quos quando lavari debeant, quando natare, quando cenare alius admonet: usque eo nimio delicati animi languore soluuntur, ut per se scire non possint an esuriant. Audio quendam ex delicatis (si modo deliciae vocandae sunt vitam et consuetudinem humanam dediscere), cum ex balneo inter manus elatus et in sella positus esset, dixisse interrogando: "Iam sedeo?" Hunc tu ignorantem an sedeat putas scire an vivat, an videat, an otiosus sit? Non facile dixerim utrum magis miserear, si hoc ignoravit an si ignorare se

right on time for their rides as though they were forbidden to miss them, who have to be told by another what time to bathe, to swim, or to eat; they've become so lax, through too much idleness of their overindulged minds, that they can't tell, on their own, whether they're hungry.

I've even heard tell of one of these overindulged—if you can call it "indulgence" to unlearn human life and practice—who, when he'd been carried from his bath by his porters' hands and placed in his sedan chair, asked, "Am I seated now?" Do you think the man who didn't know if he was sitting will know whether he's living? Or seeing? Or whether he's at leisure? I can't say for sure whether I'd pity him more if he really didn't know this or only pretended not to know. Such people genuinely feel insensible to many things, but they also feign

finxit. Multarum quidem rerum oblivionem sentiunt, sed multarum et imitantur; quaedam vitia illos quasi felicitatis argumenta delectant; nimis humilis et contempti hominis videtur scire quid facias: i nunc et mimos multa mentiri ad exprobrandam luxuriam puta. Plura me hercules praetereunt quam fingunt et tanta incredibilium vitiorum copia ingenioso in hoc unum saeculo processit, ut iam mimorum arguere possimus neglegentiam. Esse aliquem qui usque eo deliciis interierit ut an sedeat alteri credat! Non est ergo hic otiosus, aliud illi nomen imponas; aeger est, immo mortuus est; ille otiosus est cui otii sui et sensus est. Hic vero semiviuus, cui ad intellegendos corporis sui habitus indice opus est,

insensibility. A certain amount of vice gives them pleasure, supplying as it were a proof of their prosperity; it's the mark of the lowly and base to seem to know what they're doing.

Just suppose—ha!—that mimes[36] perform their many made-up dramas with the goal of attacking luxuriousness. By Hercules, they pass over more things than they invent; so great a bounty of outrageous vices has been devised, in an age that's ingenious at this one thing: leaving mimes open to being attacked for neglect. That someone could exist so far gone in luxury that he relies on another to tell him whether he's seated! This man is not at leisure, no; you must give him another label—he's ill; no, rather, he's dead. It's those who are aware of their own leisure who truly have leisure. Whereas this half-living soul, who needs a sign to show him

quomodo potest hic ullius temporis dominus esse?

XIII. Persequi singulos longum est quorum aut latrunculi aut pila aut excoquendi in sole corporis cura consumpsere vitam. Non sunt otiosi quorum voluptates multum negotii habent. Nam de illis nemo dubitabit quin operose nihil agant, qui litterarum inutilium studiis detinentur, quae iam apud Romanos quoque magna manus est. Graecorum iste morbus fuit quaerere quem numerum Ulixes remigum habuisset, prior scripta esset Ilias an Odyssia, praeterea an eiusdem esset auctoris, alia deinceps huius notae, quae sive contineas nihil tacitam conscientiam iuuant, sive proferas non doctior videaris sed

the posture of his own body—how can *he* be the master of any portion of time?

[13] It's a big task to recount individual cases: people whose lives are spent on game-board pieces, on balls, or on zealously baking their bodies in the sun. You can't say they're at leisure if their diversions entail the opposite of leisure.

No one can doubt that those who keep busy studying useless literature expend a lot of effort for no accomplishment. By this time there's a huge crowd of these types here at Rome. It used to be a disease of the *Greeks* to ask how many oarsmen Odysseus had, or which was written first, the *Iliad* or the *Odyssey*, or whether both poems came from the same author,[37] and other questions of that type, things that don't increase your own sense of your learning if you keep them to yourself, but if you share

molestior. Ecce Romanos quoque invasit inane studium supervacua discendi; his diebus audivi quendam referentem quae primus quisque ex Romanis ducibus fecisset: primus navali proelio Duilius vicit, primus Curius Dentatus in triumpho duxit elephantos. Etiamnunc ista, etsi ad veram gloriam non tendunt, circa civilium tamen operum exempla versantur; non est profutura talis scientia, est tamen quae nos speciosa rerum vanitate detineat. Hoc quoque quaerentibus remittamus quis Romanis primus persuaserit navem conscendere (Claudius is fuit, Caudex ob hoc ipsum appellatus quia plurium tabularum contextus caudex apud antiquos vocatur, unde publicae tabulae

them, make you seem tedious rather than learned. But look! Now the hollow zeal for learning meaningless things has taken the *Romans*, too, by storm. Just recently I heard someone recount what each Roman leader had been first to achieve:[38] Duilius was the first to win a battle at sea; Curius Dentatus was the first to parade elephants in a triumphal procession. These things at least have some connection to the public good, even if they don't incline toward true glory. But this kind of research will not benefit us; it diverts us with content that's empty but attractive.

Let's excuse also the people who look into the following: who it was that first persuaded the Romans to form a navy (it was Claudius "Caudex," so called for the following reason—a structure joined together by a number of pieces of wood used to be called

codices dicuntur et naves nunc quoque ex
antiqua consuetudine quae commeatus per
Tiberim subvehunt codicariae vocantur);
sane et hoc ad rem pertineat, quod Valerius Corvinus primus Messanam vicit et
primus ex familia Valeriorum, urbis captae
in se translato nomine, Messana appellatus
est paulatimque vulgo permutante litteras
Messala dictus: num et hoc cuiquam curare
permittes quod primus L. Sulla in circo le-
ones solutos dedit, cum alioquin alligati
darentur, ad conficiendos eos missis a rege
Boccho iaculatoribus? Et hoc sane remitta-
tur: num et Pompeium primum in circo

a *caudex*. Hence, collections of public documents are called *codices*, and even today ships that ply upriver on the Tiber with their cargoes are called *codicariae*, after the ancient usage). No doubt the following, too, has some point: Valerius Corvinus first conquered Messana in Sicily and became the first of the Valerii to be called Messana after the name of the captured city, but little by little came to be called Messalla as popular usage altered the name. But surely you won't allow anyone to look into *this*: the fact that Lucius Sulla first put lions roaming free on show in the Circus, though they'd been shown at other times bound with ropes, and that King Bocchus of North Africa sent javelin-men to finish them off? Perhaps that, too, might be excused. But surely *this* serves no good purpose: Pompey was the first to put on in the Circus a fight against eighteen

elephantorum duodeviginti pugnam ed-
idisse commissis more proelii noxiis hominibus, ad ullam rem bonam pertinet? Prin-
ceps civitatis et inter antiquos principes (ut
fama tradidit) bonitatis eximiae memorabile
putavit spectaculi genus novo more perdere
homines. "Depugnant? Parum est. Lanci-
nantur? Parum est: ingenti mole animalium
exterantur!" Satius erat ista in oblivionem ire,
ne quis postea potens disceret invideretque
rei minime humanae. O quantum caliginis
mentibus nostris obicit magna felicitas! Ille
se supra rerum naturam esse tunc credidit,
cum tot miserorum hominum catervas sub
alio caelo natis beluis obiceret, cum bellum
inter tam disparia animalia committeret,

elephants, assigning men who were not even guilty of crimes to do battle, as it were, against them. (Pompey, a leader of the state and, as we learn from report, a man who stood out for virtue among leaders of old, thought it a memorable kind of spectacle to destroy human beings in a novel manner! "They're fighting to the death? Not enough! They're cut to ribbons? Not enough! Let's see them pulverized by mountainous beasts!" Better that things such as that be forgotten, lest some later strongman come to learn of it and envy a thing so lacking humanity. Alas! How great success brings a fog to our minds! Pompey thought he'd surpassed the natural order at the moment when he was throwing so many gangs of wretched men to monstrous beasts born in foreign lands, when he was causing such disparate species to do battle, when he was

cum in conspectum populi Romani multum sanguinis funderet mox plus ipsum
fundere coacturus; at idem postea Alexan-
drina perfidia deceptus ultimo mancipio
transfodiendum se praebuit, tum demum
intellecta inani iactatione cognominis sui.
Sed, ut illo revertar unde decessi et in eadem
materia ostendam supervacuam quorundam diligentiam, idem narrabat Metellum,
victis in Sicilia Poenis triumphantem,
unum omnium Romanorum ante currum
centum et viginti captivos elephantos dux-
isse; Sullam ultimum Romanorum protulisse
pomerium, quod numquam provinciali sed
Italico agro adquisito proferre moris apud

spilling copious blood before the eyes of the Roman people, even as he prepared to force that very people to shed more blood. Yet later this same Pompey, deceived by Egyptian treachery, laid himself open to being run through by his lowest henchman,[39] at last learning the hollowness of the boast his surname, "the Great," contained.)

But to return to the point from which I digressed and to show that the effort some people expend on these topics is useless: the same person I mentioned earlier tells us that Metellus, after his defeat of the Carthaginians in Sicily, was the only Roman to have 120 captive elephants led before his chariot in his triumphal procession; and that Sulla was the last of the Romans to extend the circuit of the pomerium, which according to long-standing custom was extended only when Italian land, not land in the provinces,

antiquos fuit. Hoc scire magis prodest quam
Aventinum montem extra pomerium esse, ut
ille affirmabat, propter alteram ex duabus
causis, aut quod plebs eo secessisset aut
quod Remo auspicanti illo loco aves non
addixissent, alia deinceps innumerabilia
quae aut farta sunt mendaciis aut similia?
Nam ut concedas omnia eos fide bona dicere, ut ad praestationem scribant, tamen
cuius ista errores minuent? cuius cupiditates
prement? quem fortiorem, quem iustiorem,
quem liberaliorem facient? Dubitare se interim Fabianus noster aiebat an satius esset
nullis studiis admoveri quam his implicari.

was acquired. It's more beneficial to know this than the fact that the Aventine Hill is outside the pomerium, as our author asserts, for one of two reasons: either because the common people chose to secede to that spot or because the birds there had not been auspicious when Remus was watching for bird signs; and other countless things beyond that, either jam-packed with falsehoods or like falsehoods themselves.

Even if you grant that antiquarians tell us all these things with good intentions, even if they pledge that their writings are true, still, whose mistakes are diminished by their information? Whose yearnings will they suppress? Whom will they make braver, more just, or more generous? Our Fabianus[40] used to say that he was uncertain whether it was better not to devote oneself to *any*

XIV. Soli omnium otiosi sunt qui sapientiae vacant, soli viuunt; nec enim suam tantum aetatem bene tuentur: omne aeuum suo adiciunt; quicquid annorum ante illos actum est, illis adquisitum est. Nisi ingratissimi sumus, illi clarissimi sacrarum opinionum conditores nobis nati sunt, nobis vitam praeparaverunt. Ad res pulcherrimas ex tenebris ad lucem erutas alieno labore deducimur; nullo nobis saeculo interdictum est, in omnia admittimur et, si magnitudine animi egredi humanae imbecillitatis angustias libet, multum per quod spatiemur temporis est. Disputare cum Socrate licet,

field of study than to get involved with *these* fields.

[14] The only people enjoying true leisure are those who make time for philosophy.[41] Only *they* are truly alive. They not only attend to their own life span but add every age to their own. Whatever portion of time has passed before they came on the scene is annexed to their stretch of time. If we're not terribly lacking in gratitude, those most illustrious founders of sanctified schools of thought were born for *our* sake; for *us* they fashioned a paradigm of true life. We are led by others' efforts toward finer matters, things dragged out of the shadows and into the light. From no century are we barred; we're admitted to all of them. If through breadth of mind we're permitted to transcend the narrowness of human frailty, there's a huge span of time available

dubitare cum Carneade, cum Epicuro qui-
escere, hominis naturam cum Stoicis vin-
cere, cum Cynicis excedere. Cum rerum
natura in consortium omnis aevi patiatur
incedere, quidni ab hoc exiguo et caduco
temporis transitu in illa toto nos demus
animo quae immensa, quae aeterna sunt,
quae cum melioribus communia? Isti qui
per officia discursant, qui se aliosque inqui-
etant, cum bene insanierint, cum omnium
limina cotidie perambulaverint nec ullas ap-
ertas fores praeterierint, cum per diversis-
simas domos meritoriam salutationem cir-
cumtulerint, quotum quemque ex tam
immensa et variis cupiditatibus districta
urbe poterunt videre? Quam multi erunt

for us to roam through. One can argue with Socrates, entertain doubts with Carneades, be at peace along with Epicurus, overcome human nature with the Stoics, surpass it with the Cynics.[42] Since Nature permits us to enter a shared reservoir of all time, why do we not commit ourselves with our entire mind to leaving this small and transitory passage of time and going to times that are vast, eternal, and shared with those better than we are?

Those people who trot about on their errands,[43] who vex themselves and vex others, when they've thoroughly indulged their madness, when they've circled past every threshold on their daily rounds and yet passed by not a single open door, when they've given their money-grubbing greeting at houses far and wide, how few of their patrons will they be able to spot, in so vast

quorum illos aut somnus aut luxuria aut in-
humanitas summoveat! Quam multi qui
illos, cum diu torserint, simulata festina-
tione transcurrant! Quam multi per refer-
tum clientibus atrium prodire vitabunt et
per obscuros aedium aditus profugient,
quasi non inhumanius sit decipere quam
excludere! Quam multi hesterna crapula
semisomnes et graves illis miseris suum
somnum rumpentibus ut alienum exspec-
tent, vix allevatis labris insusurratum miliens
nomen oscitatione superbissima reddent!
Hos in veris officiis morari putamus? Immo
id facere illos potius licet dicamus qui Zeno-
nem, qui Pythagoran cotidie et Democri-
tum ceterosque antistites bonarum artium,

a city, so divided by desires of all kinds!
How many the patrons whose sleep or over-
indulgence or coldness dispels their clients!
How many have tortured their clients with
long delays, then run past them in pretended
haste! How many will avoid going out
through an atrium packed with clients but
escape through the house's hidden passage-
ways, as though it were not colder to deceive
them than to hold them at arm's length!
How many, still half-asleep from yester-
day's bender and groggy, will address those
who've interrupted their own sleep in order
to wait while another finishes his, using a
name spoken to them a thousand times by
lips that scarcely move,[44] but delivering it
with an extremely haughty yawn!

Do we suppose that these people are
spending time in true pursuits? We might
rather say that of those who, every day, want

qui Aristotelen et Theophrastum volent habere quam familiarissimos. Nemo horum non vacabit, nemo non venientem ad se beatiorem, amantiorem sui dimittet, nemo quemquam vacuis a se manibus abire patietur; nocte conveniri, interdiu ab omnibus mortalibus possunt.

XV. Horum te mori nemo coget, omnes docebunt; horum nemo annos tuos conterit, suos tibi contribuit; nullius ex his sermo periculosus erit, nullius amicitia capitalis, nullius sumptuosa observatio. Feres ex illis quicquid voles; per illos non stabit quominus quantum plurimum cupieris haurias.

to have Zeno, Pythagoras, Democritus, as their most intimate friends, and other high priests of good arts, and Aristotle, and Theophrastus. None of these will be too busy; none will fail to send back the visitor happier and fonder of himself; none will allow anyone to go away empty-handed. These can be approached by anyone, nighttime or daytime.

[15] None of these will compel you to die, but all will teach you how to do it.[45] None will take away from your store of years, but each will add his own to increase that store. None will endanger you because you engaged them in conversation; none offers a friendship that might cost you your head;[46] none demands you attend him at exorbitant expense. You'll take from them whatever you desire. They won't be to blame if you don't absorb every last drop you have

Quae illum felicitas, quam pulchra senectus
manet, qui se in horum clientelam contulit!
Habebit cum quibus de minimis maximisque
rebus deliberet, quos de se cotidie consulat,
a quibus audiat verum sine contumelia, lau-
detur sine adulatione, ad quorum se simili-
tudinem effingat. Solemus dicere non
fuisse in nostra potestate quos sortiremur
parentes, forte nobis datos: bonis vero ad
suum arbitrium nasci licet. Nobilissimo-
rum ingeniorum familiae sunt: elige in
quam adscisci velis; non in nomen tantum
adoptaberis, sed in ipsa bona, quae non
erunt sordide nec maligne custodienda:
maiora fient quo illa pluribus diviseris. Hi
tibi dabunt ad aeternitatem iter et te in illum

room for. What happiness, what a fine old age, awaits those who make themselves clients of *these* people! They'll have those with whom to deliberate about small matters and great; to consult every day about their own condition; to get the truth from, without taking offense; to furnish a model for their self-fashioning.

We often say that we had no power to choose our parents and that these were given to us by chance, but we can in fact be born to whomever we want. There are families out there made up of the noblest intellects; pick the one you want to be joined with. You will be adopted by taking on not only their name but also their goods,[47] which you must not guard in a cheap or mean-spirited way—they'll grow greater the more widely you share them. It's these people who'll put you on the path toward eternity and raise

locum ex quo nemo deicitur sublevabunt.
Haec una ratio est extendendae mortalitatis,
immo in immortalitatem vertendae. Honores, monumenta, quicquid aut decretis
ambitio iussit aut operibus exstruxit cito
subruitur, nihil non longa demolitur vetus-
tas et movet; at iis quae consecravit sapien-
tia nocere non potest; nulla abolebit aetas,
nulla deminuet; sequens ac deinde semper
ulterior aliquid ad venerationem conferet,
quoniam quidem in vicino versatur invidia,
simplicius longe posita miramur. Sapientis
ergo multum patet vita; non idem illum qui
ceteros terminus cludit; solus generis hu-
mani legibus soluitur; omnia illi saecula ut
deo serviunt. Transiit tempus aliquod? hoc

you to a place from which no one can be cast down.

This is the one way of lengthening human life—nay, of changing mortality into immortality. Honors, monuments, and whatever our strivings have gotten passed by decree or built by effort are quickly destroyed; nothing exists that the world's old age doesn't wreck or transform. But the things made holy by wisdom can't be harmed. No span of time will erase them or diminish them; the next span, and the next, will add to their honor (since we tend to begrudge things closest to ourselves but marvel more freely at those that lie far off).

That's why the life of philosophers spreads wide and the boundaries that enclose others don't limit *them*. They alone are exempt from the laws that govern the human race. All ages obey them as though

recordatione comprendit; instat? hoc utitur; venturum est? hoc praecipit. Longam illi vitam facit omnium temporum in unum collatio.

XVI. Illorum brevissima ac sollicitissima aetas est qui praeteritorum obliviscuntur, praesentia neglegunt, de futuro timent: cum ad extrema venerunt, sero intellegunt miseri tam diu se dum nihil agunt occupatos fuisse. Nec est quod hoc argumento probari putes longam illos agere vitam, quia interdum mortem invocant: vexat illos imprudentia incertis affectibus et incurrentibus in ipsa quae metuunt; mortem saepe ideo optant quia timent. Illud quoque argumentum non

obeying a god. The time that's passing is stamped in their memory; the time that's upon them they put to good use; the time that's to come they anticipate. By combining all times into one, they make their life long.

[16] Shortest and most troubled of all lives are those of people who forget the past, disregard the present, and fear the future. When they've reached the final stages, they understand, too late, that they had been preoccupied for so long while doing nothing at all. And you can't possibly claim that they lead a long life by arguing that they summon death from time to time.[18] That's only because lack of awareness, with shifting emotions that rush headlong toward the very things they fear, disturbs them, so they often long for death because they fear it. And this, too, you should not regard as an

est quod putes diu viventium, quod saepe
illis longus videtur dies, quod, dum veniat
condictum tempus cenae, tarde ire horas
queruntur; nam si quando illos deseruerunt
occupationes, in otio relicti aestuant nec
quomodo id disponant ut extrahant sciunt.
Itaque ad occupationem aliquam tendunt et
quod interiacet omne tempus grave est, tam
me hercules quam cum dies muneris gladi-
atorii edictus est, aut cum alicuius alterius
vel spectaculi vel voluptatis exspectatur
constitutum, transilire medios dies volunt.
Omnis illis speratae rei longa dilatio est; at
illud tempus quod amant breve est et praeceps breviusque multo, suo vitio; aliunde
enim alio transfugiunt et consistere in una

argument that they live long: the fact that the day often seems long to them and that until the appointed hour of dinner arrives, they complain that the hours are crawling. It's only because when their distractions have abandoned them, they're all in a lather, left in a state of leisure that they don't know how to either use or extend. So they move on to some other distraction and all the intervening time becomes a burden, just like (by Hercules!) when the date of a gladiatorial show has been proclaimed, or when the appointed time of some other spectacle or delight is anticipated, they want to leap past the intervening days.

Every delay of something they hope for seems long to them. But the time they spend in enjoyment seems short; it rushes past, more fleeting because of their own failing, for they dash here and there, from one

cupiditate non possunt. Non sunt illis longi dies, sed invisi; at contra quam exiguae noctes videntur, quas in complexu scortorum aut vino exigunt! Inde etiam poetarum furor fabulis humanos errores alentium, quibus visus est Iuppiter voluptate concubitus delenitus duplicasse noctem; quid aliud est vitia nostra incendere quam auctores illis inscribere deos et dare morbo exemplo divinitatis excusatam licentiam? Possunt istis non brevissimae videri noctes quas tam care mercantur? Diem noctis exspectatione perdunt, noctem lucis metu.

XVII. Ipsae voluptates eorum trepidae et variis terroribus inquietae sunt subitque cum maxime exsultantis sollicita cogitatio:

pursuit to another, and they can't stay put in any one desire. Their days aren't long but hateful. But then, how short their nights seem, spent in the embraces of whores and in wine! Thus comes the insanity of poets who nurture human misdeeds with their stories; they envision Jupiter, softened by the pleasure of lovemaking, doubling the length of the night.[49] What else would you call this kindling of our vices, other than making the gods their founders and giving excuse and license to our illness by way of divine precedent?

Can nights that are bought at so high a price seem anything but short to these people? They squander the day in awaiting the night and the night in fearing the day.

[17] The very pleasures these people enjoy are filled with anxiety and disturbed by all kinds of fears. A troubling thought steals

"Haec quam diu?" Ab hoc affectu reges suam flevere potentiam, nec illos magnitudo fortunae suae delectavit, sed venturus aliquando finis exterruit. Cum per magna camporum spatia porrigeret exercitum nec numerum eius sed mensuram comprenderet Persarum rex insolentissimus, lacrimas profudit, quod intra centum annos nemo ex tanta iuventute superfuturus esset; at illis admoturus erat fatum ipse qui flebat perditurusque alios in mari alios in terra, alios proelio alios fuga, et intra exiguum tempus consumpturus illos quibus centesimum

upon them just when they're rejoicing: "How long will this last?" Kings have wept over their own power when this emotion has come over them; the greatness of their high state doesn't delight them, but the end-point, sure to arrive at some time, terrifies them. The Great King of Persia, a very arrogant man, when he had spread out his army through huge expanses of ground, counting them by means of the space they occupied rather than by number, shed tears because no one among that vast array of youth would be alive in a hundred years.[50] Yet the very man who wept was about to bring their fate on them and destroy some on the sea, others on land, others in combat, others in flight; he'd destroy in a short space of time those whose hundredth year he feared for.

annum timebat. Quid quod gaudia quoque
eorum trepida sunt? Non enim solidis causis innituntur, sed eadem qua oriuntur vanitate turbantur. Qualia autem putas esse
tempora etiam ipsorum confessione misera,
cum haec quoque quibus se attollunt et
super hominem efferunt parum sincera sint?
Maxima quaeque bona sollicita sunt nec ulli
fortunae minus bene quam optimae credi-
tur; alia felicitate ad tuendam felicitatem
opus est et pro ipsis quae successere votis
vota facienda sunt. Omne enim quod fortuito obuenit instabile est: quod altius surrex-
erit, opportunius est in occasum. Neminem
porro casura delectant; miserrimam ergo

And what about this: even the *joys* of these people are filled with anxiety. For the causes these joys rely on are unstable; the hollowness that they emerged from makes them chaotic. What sort of bad times do you think these people are having when they admit they're unhappy, since their *good* times, in which they exalt themselves and raise themselves up to superhuman levels, are a very mixed lot?

All the greatest joys are attended by worry. No fortune is less wisely trusted than the best kind. One needs another happiness to safeguard the happiness one has; prayers need to be made on behalf of prayers already fulfilled. Everything that comes about by chance is unsteady; the higher it rises, the more susceptible it is to a fall. And since things that are destined to fall give no delight, it's inevitable that the life of those

necesse est, non tantum brevissimam vitam
esse eorum qui magno parant labore quod
maiore possideant. Operose assequuntur
quae volunt, anxii tenent quae assecuti sunt;
nulla interim numquam amplius redituri
temporis ratio est: novae occupationes vet-
eribus substituuntur, spes spem excitat,
ambitionem ambitio. Miseriarum non finis
quaeritur, sed materia mutatur. Nostri nos
honores torserunt? plus temporis alieni
auferunt; candidati laborare desiimus? suf-
fragatores incipimus; accusandi deposuimus
molestiam? iudicandi nanciscimur; iudex
desiit esse? quaesitor est; alienorum bono-
rum mercennaria procuratione consenuit?

who get with much effort what they hold on to with *more* must be not only extremely short but extremely unhappy. They laboriously acquire what they want and then cling anxiously to their acquisitions; meanwhile they take no account of the *time* they'll never get back. New distractions replace old ones; a first hope arouses a second; a first goal, a second. No endpoint of miseries is looked for, only a change of their content. The offices we've held have brought us torment? Those held by others take *more* of our time. We've ceased from the toil of candidacy? Now we start the toil of canvassing. We've left aside the nuisance of prosecuting? We've taken up that of a judgeship. The judge is no longer a judge; now he heads a commission. The man who's grown old looking after another's estate, a steward for

suis opibus distinetur. Marium caliga dimisit? consulatus exercet; Quintius dictaturam properat pervadere? ab aratro revocabitur. Ibit in Poenos nondum tantae maturus rei Scipio; victor Hannibalis victor Antiochi, sui consulatus decus fraterni sponsor, ni per ipsum mora esset, cum Iove reponeretur: civiles servatorem agitabunt seditiones et post fastiditos a iuvene diis aequos honores iam senem contumacis exilii delectabit ambitio. Numquam derunt vel felices vel miserae sollicitudinis causae; per occupationes vita trudetur; otium numquam agetur, semper optabitur.

hire, turns his gaze instead to his own property.

Marius took off his soldier's boots and took up the consulship. Cincinnatus hastens to discharge his dictator's powers, but he'll be called back from his plow. Scipio will take on Carthage, though not yet prepared for such a great task; he'll defeat Hannibal and Antiochus, win glory for his own consulship, and guarantee that of his brother; he'll be placed next to Jupiter, except for the halt he himself called.[51] Even so, civil discord will trouble the state's savior,[52] and after scorning in youth the honors that equaled the gods, as an old man he'll delight in a show of proud exile. There will always be reasons for worry, whether they spring from good fortune or bad. Life will be thrust onward from one pursuit to the next.

XVIII. Excerpe itaque te vulgo, Pauline carissime, et in tranquilliorem portum non pro aetatis spatio iactatus tandem recede. Cogita quot fluctus subieris, quot tempestates partim privatas sustinueris, partim publicas in te converteris; satis iam per laboriosa et inquieta documenta exhibita virtus est; experire quid in otio faciat. Maior pars aetatis, certe melior rei publicae datast: aliquid temporis tui sume etiam tibi. Nec te ad segnem aut inertem quietem voco, non ut somno et caris turbae voluptatibus quicquid

Leisure will never be obtained but always longed for.

[18] So detach yourself from the crowd, my dearest Paulinus, and withdraw to a more peaceful harbor, after being tossed about in a way that doesn't square with your age.[53] Consider how many waves you've weathered and how many storms you've ridden out as a private citizen and how many you've brought on yourself in public office. Your virtue has been enough demonstrated by now, by way of toilsome, unceasing proofs; try out what it can accomplish in retirement. The greater part of your life, certainly the better part, has been given to the state;[54] take some portion of your time for yourself as well.

I'm not summoning you to a slothful or idle rest, to drown whatever lively spirit you have in sleep and in the pleasures valued by

est in te indolis vividae mergas; non est istud
adquiescere: invenies maiora omnibus adhuc
strenue tractatis operibus, quae repositus et
securus agites. Tu quidem orbis terrarum
rationes administras tam abstinenter quam
alienas, tam diligenter quam tuas, tam
religiose quam publicas. In officio amorem
consequeris, in quo odium vitare difficile
est; sed tamen, mihi crede, satius est vitae
suae rationem quam frumenti publici nosse.
Istum animi vigorem rerum maximarum
capacissimum a ministerio honorifico quidem sed parum ad beatam vitam apto revoca, et cogita non id egisse te ab aetate prima
omni cultu studiorum liberalium ut tibi
multa milia frumenti bene committerentur;

the masses; *that's* not what I mean by repose. You'll find things to pursue, when you're secluded and freed from care, even greater than all those endeavors you've managed up to now with such great effort. You oversee the accounts of the whole world[55] as meticulously as you would those of strangers, as carefully as your own, as dutifully as those of the public; you garner love in an office in which it's hard to avoid hatred. Nonetheless, believe me, it's better to take account of one's own life than that of the grain supply. Call back that strength of mind that's most capable of the greatest things from an official post that brings honor but is not suited to a happy life; consider that you didn't make it your goal, by studying the liberal arts from earliest youth, that many thousands of measures of grain be well assigned to your care. You had raised

maius quiddam et altius de te promiseras.
Non derunt et frugalitatis exactae homines
et laboriosae operae; tanto aptiora portan-
dis oneribus tarda iumenta sunt quam nobiles equi, quorum generosam pernicitatem
quis umquam gravi sarcina pressit? Cogita
praeterea quantum sollicitudinis sit ad tan-
tam te molem obicere: cum ventre tibi hu-
mano negotium est; nec rationem patitur nec
aequitate mitigatur nec ulla prece flectitur
populus esuriens. Modo modo intra paucos illos dies quibus C. Caesar periit (si
quis inferis sensus est) hoc gravissime ferens
quod decedebat populo Romano superstite,
septem aut octo certe dierum cibaria superesse! Dum ille pontes navibus iungit et viri-
bus imperi ludit, aderat ultimum malorum

hopes that something higher and greater was coming from you. There's no lack of men who have both scrupulous and diligent characters. Sluggish pack animals are more suited to carrying burdens than purebred steeds, for who ever weighed down the speed of the latter with heavy loads?

Consider also how fretful it is to take on yourself such a great burden. Your dealings are with the human stomach. A hungry populace doesn't listen to reason; it's not appeased by fair treatment or moved by entreaty. Just recently, in the few days following the death of Caligula—who was taking it very badly (if the dead have any feelings) that, as he could see, the surviving Roman populace had food left for seven or eight days[56]—there was a scarcity of food, the worst of evils even for those under siege, on top of his building bridges of boats and

obsessis quoque, alimentorum egestas; exitio paene ac fame constitit et, quae famem sequitur, rerum omnium ruina furiosi et externi et infeliciter superbi regis imitatio. Quem tunc animum habuerunt illi quibus erat mandata frumenti publici cura, saxa, ferrum, ignes, Gaium excepturi? Summa dissimulatione tantum inter viscera latentis mali tegebant, cum ratione scilicet: quaedam enim ignorantibus aegris curanda sunt, causa multis moriendi fuit morbum suum nosse.

XIX. Recipe te ad haec tranquilliora, tutiora, maiora! Simile tu putas esse, utrum cures ut incorruptum et a fraude advehentium et a neglegentia frumentum transfundatur in horrea, ne concepto umore vitietur

sporting with the empire's assets.[57] His imitation of an insane and foreign and ill-starred, arrogant king ended up in near death by starvation and, as a sequel to famine, universal destruction. What did they feel then, those who'd been put in charge of the public grain stores, when they were destined to endure stones, swords, fires, Caligula? With the height of deception, they covered up the great evil lurking in the state's innards, and with good reason, to be sure (for some illnesses have to be cured while those who ail are as yet unaware; in many cases the knowledge of the disease has been the cause of death).

[19] Return yourself to these more serene, more secure, and more important things. Do you think these things are on an equal footing: whether you take care that the grain gets poured into the storeroom undamaged

et concalescat, ut ad mensuram pondusque respondeat, an ad haec sacra et sublimia accedas sciturus quae materia sit dei, quae voluptas, quae condicio, quae forma; quis animum tuum casus exspectet; ubi nos a corporibus dimissos natura componat; quid sit quod huius mundi gravissima quaeque in medio sustineat, supra levia suspendat, in summum ignem ferat, sidera vicibus suis excitet; cetera deinceps ingentibus plena miraculis? Vis tu relicto solo mente ad ista respicere! Nunc, dum calet sanguis, ad meliora eundum est. Exspectat te in hoc genere

by the deceit of pilferers or by neglect, that it not get spoiled by moisture or overheated, that it tallies up according to weight and measure; or whether you occupy yourself with these holy and sublime things: the intent to find out what godhead is made of, what its will is, what character and form it possesses, what outcome awaits your soul, where Nature places us once we're released from our bodies, what it is that keeps all the heaviest parts of this universe centered, hangs the lighter parts on high, brings fire up to the top, stirs the heavenly bodies to go through their changes—to find out other things too, in their turn, all filled with vast miracles? Don't you want to leave the dull clay and cast your mind's eye toward these things? Now, while your heart is still thumping,[58] the journey to better things must be undertaken. In this mode of life,

vitae multum bonarum artium, amor virtu-
tum atque usus, cupiditatum oblivio, vivendi
ac moriendi scientia, alta rerum quies. Omnium quidem occupatorum condicio misera
est, eorum tamen miserrima, qui ne suis
quidem laborant occupationibus, ad alienum dormiunt somnum, ad alienum ambu-
lant gradum, amare et odisse, res omnium
liberrimas, iubentur. Hi si volent scire quam
brevis ipsorum vita sit, cogitent ex quota
parte sua sit.

XX. Cum videris itaque praetextam saepe
iam sumptam, cum celebre in foro nomen,
ne invideris: ista vitae damno parantur.
Vt unus ab illis numeretur annus, omnis annos suos conterent. Quosdam antequam in

there awaits you a great array of good arts: the love and the practice of virtues, nonconsciousness of the passions, knowledge of living and dying, deep respite from wordly affairs.

All those who are preoccupied are in a wretched state, but wretchedest are those who struggle with preoccupations that are not even their own; they sleep in step with the sleep of another, they walk at another's pace.[59] They're under orders as to their loves and hates, the freest of all things. If they want to know how short their own life is, they should consider how small a part of it is their own.

[20] So then, whenever you see a magistrate's toga put on many times,[60] or a name that's well-known in the Forum, don't be jealous. These things are obtained at the cost of one's life. To get their name on a single

summum ambitionis eniterentur, inter prima luctantis aetas reliquit; quosdam, cum in consummationem dignitatis per mille indignitates erepsissent, misera subiit cogitatio laborasse ipsos in titulum sepulcri; quorundam ultima senectus, dum in novas spes ut iuventa disponitur, inter conatus magnos et improbos invalida defecit. Foedus ille quem in iudicio pro ignotissimis litigatoribus grandem natu et imperitae coronae assensiones captantem spiritus liquit; turpis ille qui vivendo lassus citius quam laborando inter ipsa officia collapsus est; turpis quem accipiendis immorientem rationibus diu tractus risit heres. Praeterire

year, they'll wear away all their years.[61] Some are abandoned by life amid their first strivings, before they can struggle up to the peak of ambition; others, after they've clawed their way up through a thousand indignities to the heights of dignity, are struck by the awful thought that they've only been toiling to carve their own epitaph; still others find that their final old age, even as it sets out new hopes for itself as though still in youth, loses strength and gives out amid great, overreaching endeavors.

Vile are those elderly who, in the midst of a trial, aiding defendants they don't know at all, give up the ghost even as they win the applause of the courtroom; disgraceful are those who, worn out by the length of life rather than by work and effort, drop dead in the midst of their duties; disgraceful too are those who die while going over accounts

quod mihi occurrit exemplum non possum:
C. Turannius fuit exactae diligentiae senex,
qui post annum nonagesimum, cum vacationem procurationis ab C. Caesare ultro
accepisset, componi se in lecto et velut exa-
nimem a circumstante familia plangi iussit.
Lugebat domus otium domini senis nec fini-
vit ante tristitiam quam labor illi suus resti-
tutus est. Adeone iuuat occupatum mori?
Idem plerisque animus est; diutius cupiditas
illis laboris quam facultas est; cum imbecil-
litate corporis pugnant, senectutem ipsam
nullo alio nomine gravem iudicant quam
quod illos seponit. Lex a quinquagesimo

and give their long-delayed heirs a reason for laughter.

I can't resist an example that comes to my mind. Gaius Turannius[62] was an old man of proven diligence. After his ninetieth year, when he'd finally been granted a release from his procuratorship[63] by Caligula, he bid that he be stretched out on a bier and mourned by his household as they stood around him, as though he were dead. The whole house mourned the retirement of the aged master and didn't finish until his job was restored to him.

Was it really so pleasant to die while still busy? Many share this way of thinking. Their desire for work lasts longer than their strength to carry it out. They fight against the debility of the body, and they deem old age to be a burden for no other reason than that it takes them out of the game. The law

anno militem non legit, a sexagesimo sena-
torem non citat: difficilius homines a se
otium impetrant quam a lege. Interim dum
rapiuntur et rapiunt, dum alter alterius
quietem rumpit, dum mutuo miseri sunt,
vita est sine fructu, sine voluptate, sine ullo
profectu animi; nemo in conspicuo mortem
habet, nemo non procul spes intendit,
quidam vero disponunt etiam illa quae ultra
vitam sunt, magnas moles sepulcrorum et
operum publicorum dedicationes et ad
rogum munera et ambitiosas exsequias. At
me hercules istorum funera, tamquam minimum vixerint, ad faces et cereos ducenda
sunt.

exempts a soldier from service after age fifty, a senator from the roll call after age sixty; but the law grants people retirement more easily than they do themselves. So long as they grab and are grabbed from, and one breaks the peace of another, and both make one another wretched, life is a thing with no profit, no pleasure, no progress of mind.

No one keeps death in view, no one stops directing hope toward a far-off goal. Some even map out the things beyond the bounds of their life: huge mountains of tombs, dedications of public works, gladiatorial fights at their funerals, processions that make a great show. But, I swear, their funerals ought to have torchlight and wax tapers instead, as if they were dying in childhood.[64]

Moral Epistle 1

Seven years or more after writing "On the Shortness of Life," at a time when he had partly withdrawn from politics, Seneca returned to the topic of spending time well in his Moral Epistles. This magnum opus consists of a set of letters addressed (perhaps fictively) to a friend named Lucilius, like Seneca, a wealthy man serving in Nero's regime. The value of time is the focus of the very first letter in the collection, an indication of its importance in Seneca's mind. That letter is translated below in its entirety. In it, Seneca speaks to Lucilius as though his friend had just written to him about stepping back from his duties in order to free up more time. Both men were in their sixties at this point and therefore aware of time running short.

[1] Ita fac, mi Lucili: vindica te tibi, et tempus quod adhuc aut auferebatur aut subripiebatur aut excidebat collige et serva. Persuade tibi hoc sic esse ut scribo: quaedam tempora eripiuntur nobis, quaedam subducuntur, quaedam effluunt. Turpissima tamen est iactura quae per neglegentiam fit. Et si volueris attendere, magna pars vitae elabitur male agentibus, maxima nihil agentibus, tota vita aliud agentibus. [2] Quem mihi dabis qui aliquod pretium tempori ponat, qui diem aestimet, qui intellegat se cotidie mori? In hoc enim fallimur, quod mortem

[Epistle 1] That's what you should do, Lucilius; claim yourself for yourself, and hoard the time that up to now was pilfered or seized from you or that slid from your grasp. Convince yourself that things are as I here describe them: some spaces of time are snatched from us; some are siphoned off; some seep away. But the worst loss of all comes about through neglect. Indeed, if you're paying close attention, the greatest part of life slips past for those who fail to get things done, a large part for those who do nothing, and all of it for those who do something other than what they ought.

[2] Can you show me a person who places a certain price on his time, who reckons up the value of a day, who knows he's dying every passing day? We're mistaken if we think we're looking ahead to death, since a great portion of death is already past.

prospicimus: magna pars eius iam praet-
erit; quidquid aetatis retro est mors tenet.
Fac ergo, mi Lucili, quod facere te scribis,
omnes horas complectere; sic fiet ut minus
ex crastino pendeas, si hodierno manum
inieceris. [3] Dum differtur vita transcur-
rit. Omnia, Lucili, aliena sunt, tempus tantum nostrum est; in huius rei unius fugacis
ac lubricae possessionem natura nos misit,
ex qua expellit quicumque vult. Et tanta
stultitia mortalium est ut quae minima et
vilissima sunt, certe reparabilia, imputari
sibi cum impetravere patiantur, nemo se iu-
dicet quicquam debere qui tempus accepit,
cum interim hoc unum est quod ne gratus
quidem potest reddere.

Whatever part of life is behind us is already in death's grasp.

So do what you say in your letter you're doing, Lucilius—namely, embrace every hour. The result will be that you'll depend less on tomorrow if you're taking today in your hands. While we postpone it, life is hurrying past.

[3] Nothing, Lucilius, belongs to us; only time is our own. Nature has destined us to possess this one slippery and fleeting thing, and anyone who wants can strip it from us. So great is the folly of mortals that they allow themselves to be charged for all sorts of tiny and worthless things they've obtained, things that can be easily replaced if lost, but no one who gets hold of time would think he owes anything for it. And yet, it's the only thing that not even a generous person is able to repay.

[4] Interrogabis fortasse quid ego faciam qui tibi ista praecipio. Fatebor ingenue: quod apud luxuriosum sed diligentem evenit, ratio mihi constat impensae. Non possum dicere nihil perdere, sed quid perdam et quare et quemadmodum dicam; causas paupertatis meae reddam. Sed evenit mihi quod plerisque non suo vitio ad inopiam redactis: omnes ignoscunt, nemo succurrit. [5] Quid ergo est? Non puto pauperem cui quantulumcumque superest sat est; tu tamen malo serves tua, et bono tempore incipies. Nam ut visum est maioribus nostris, "sera parsimonia in fundo est"; non enim tantum minimum in imo sed pessimum remanet. Vale.

[4] Perhaps you'll ask what I myself, the man who's sharing these lessons with you, am doing. I'll confess it freely: I balance my books, just like the extravagant man who's also careful with his outlays.[65] I can't say I don't squander anything, but I'll tell you what I squander and why and how: I'll report the causes of my impoverishment. But my case is like that of many who are reduced to poverty through no fault of their own: everyone sympathizes but no one helps.

[5] What's there to say then? I don't consider people impoverished if they think the tiny amount they still have is enough. But as for you, I'd rather you keep what is yours, and it's not too soon to begin. For, as our ancestors said, "It's too late to conserve when you're down to the dregs."[66] The last layer is not only smallest but also worst. Farewell.

Epistulae Morales XLIX

[2] Modo amisisse te videor; quid enim non "modo" est, si recorderis? Modo apud Sotionem philosophum puer sedi, modo causas agere coepi, modo desii velle agere, modo

Moral Epistle 49

Amid the 128 surviving letters in the Moral Epistles, *the theme of time, and how highly it must be valued, given the nearness of death, recurs often. One other such discussion is translated below, taken from portions (a bit more than half) of Epistle 49. In this letter Seneca writes to Lucilius after the two men had (at least notionally) shared a sojourn in Campania; Lucilius had departed first, and Seneca had seen him on his way. The letter is framed as though Seneca had written it in the moments after his friend's departure.*

[2] It seems like just now that I lost you. For what is *not* "just now," if you're calling memories to mind? "Just now" I was a boy, sitting at the feet of Sotion the philosopher;[67]

desii posse. Infinita est velocitas temporis,
quae magis apparet respicientibus. Nam ad
praesentia intentos fallit; adeo praecipitis
fugae transitus lenis est. [3] Causam huius
rei quaeris? quidquid temporis transit eodem
loco est; pariter aspicitur, una iacet; omnia
in idem profundum cadunt. Et alioqui non
possunt longa intervalla esse in ea re quae
tota brevis est. Punctum est quod vivimus
et adhuc puncto minus; sed et hoc minimum specie quadam longioris spatii natura derisit: aliud ex hoc infantiam fecit,
aliud pueritiam, aliud adulescentiam, aliud
inclinationem quandam ab adulescentia ad

"just now" I began pleading legal cases; "just now" I stopped wanting to plead them, "just now" I ceased to be able. The speed of time is infinite, as appears more clearly to those looking backward. It eludes those who are consumed with the present, so gentle is the passage of its rushing flight.

[3] Do you ask me why this is? Whatever part of time has passed by is all one; it has a uniform aspect and lies in a single grave. Everything tumbles into the same abyss. Besides, there can't be any long gaps in a thing that's altogether brief.

The time we live is just a point, and even less than a point; yet Nature mocks even this tiny point with the illusion that it's a longer stretch. She has made part of it infancy, another part childhood, another adolescence, another a kind of decline from adolescence into old age, another old age

senectutem, aliud ipsam senectutem. In quam angusto quodam quot gradus posuit! [4] Modo te prosecutus sum; et tamen hoc "modo" aetatis nostrae bona portio est, cuius brevitatem aliquando defecturam cogitemus. Non solebat mihi tam velox tempus videri: nunc incredibilis cursus apparet, sive quia admoveri lineas sentio, sive quia attendere coepi et computare damnum meum.

Eo magis itaque indignor aliquos ex hoc tempore quod sufficere ne ad necessaria quidem potest, [5] etiam si custoditum diligentissime fuerit, in supervacua maiorem partem erogare. Negat Cicero, si duplicetur sibi aetas, habiturum se tempus

itself. How many steps she has made for that transit, though its stretch is so short! [4] I escorted you on your journey just now, yet this "just now" is a huge chunk of our life span—a span we ought to realize is brief and soon to expire.

Time didn't use to seem so fleeting to me. Now, its pace seems beyond belief, either because I sense the approach of the finish line or because I've started to recognize and count up what I've lost.

[5] That's why I'm more outraged that some people spend most of this small stretch of time on empty pursuits—an amount of time that, even if it were very carefully guarded, can't accommodate even what's needed. Cicero says that even if his life span were doubled, he wouldn't have enough time to read the lyric poets. . . .

quo legat lyricos. . . . [6] Quid te torques et maceras in ea quaestione quam subtilius est contempsisse quam solvere? Securi est et ex commodo migrantis minuta conquirere: cum hostis instat a tergo et movere se iussus est miles, necessitas excutit quidquid pax otiosa collegerat. [7] Non vacat mihi verba dubie cadentia consectari et vafritiam in illis meam experiri.

Aspice qui coeant populi, quae moenia
    clusis
ferrum acuant portis.

Magno mihi animo strepitus iste belli circumsonantis exaudiendus est. [8] Demens omnibus merito viderer, si cum saxa in

[6] Why do you torment yourself and get in a stew over the sort of question that's more cleverly scorned than solved?[68] It's the place of those who have no cares, who are moving along at their ease, to explore minutiae; when the enemy's right behind and the soldier is ordered into action, necessity drives out whatever things peace and leisure had gathered.[69]

[7] I no longer have time to parse ambiguous expressions and test my wits on them.

> Look at the peoples gathered, the walls
> with their gates barred,
> the sharpened blade.[70]

That clamor of war is sounding everywhere; I need a strong mind to endure the sound. [8] I'd seem insane to everyone, with reason, if when old men and women were

munimentum murorum senes feminaeque
congererent, cum iuventus intra portas armata
signum eruptionis exspectaret aut posceret,
cum hostilia in portis tela vibrarent et ipsum
solum suffossionibus et cuniculis tremeret,
sederem otiosus et quaestiunculas ponens . . .
[9] Non vaco ad istas ineptias; ingens negotium in manibus est. Quid agam? mors me
sequitur, fugit vita. [10] Adversus haec me
doce aliquid; effice ut ego mortem non
fugiam, vita me non effugiat. Exhortare adversus difficilia, adde aequanimitatem adversus inevitabilia; angustias temporis mei
laxa. Doce non esse positum bonum vitae in
spatio eius sed in usu posse fieri, immo

hauling rocks to firm up the walls, when the younger cohort had taken up arms inside the gates and was awaiting, nay, demanding, the signal to burst out and attack, when enemy weapons are quivering as they strike the wooden gates and the very ground is quaking from the mines and tunnels dug under it—if I were then to sit at my leisure posing obscure little problems . . . [9] I have no time for such foolishness; I have a great endeavor in hand.

What am I to do? Death is pursuing me, while life flees. Teach me something to remedy this situation. [10] Make it so that I won't flee death and life won't flee me. Give me encouragement to face my hardships and calmness of mind to meet what can't be avoided. Widen the narrow space of my time. Teach me that the goodness of life does not lie in its length but in the use made of it

saepissime fieri, ut qui diu vixit parum vix-
erit. Dic mihi dormituro "potes non exper-
gisci"; dic experrecto "potes non dormire
amplius." Dic exeunti "potes non reverti";
dic redeunti "potes non exire." [11] Erras si
in navigatione tantum existimas minimum
esse quo <a> morte vita diducitur: in omni
loco aeque tenue intervallum est.

and that it can happen—very often *does* happen—that those who lived long *lived* too little. Tell me as I'm going to sleep, "You might not wake up," and tell me as I wake up, "You might not go to sleep again." Tell me as I go out, "You might not come back," and tell me as I come back, "You might never leave."

[11] You're wrong if you think that only at sea is life separated from death by a tiny distance. The gap is equally narrow everywhere.

NOTES

1. It's largely agreed that the addressee of the work was Pompeius Paulinus and that he was Seneca's father-in-law. At the time Seneca wrote, Paulinus was in his late fifties or early sixties, serving as praefectus annonae—the officer in charge of Rome's grain supply—or perhaps very recently dismissed from that post (as discussed in the introduction).
2. Hippocrates of Cos, a Greek medical writer of the fifth century BC.
3. A sentiment like this is attributed not to Aristotle but to his student Theophrastus by Cicero.
4. The quote is not metrical, as one would expect of a line of verse, and does not

correspond to anything found in Vergil or Homer, the two poets whom Seneca elsewhere describes as the "greatest."

5. Here, as often in this essay, Seneca looks askance at the Roman *clientela* system, by which *clientes*, dependents, came daily to seek favors from wealthy or powerful *patrones*. Those beset by their clientes, as was Seneca himself, are obliged to devote large stretches of time to the problems of others.

6. The "sound pursuits" will be discussed later (chapters 14–16 below), but Seneca provides a hint with his reference just above to "higher thought" (or more literally "good mind").

7. The emperor Augustus, dead for about forty years by the time of this essay, had been deified soon after his death and was worshipped as a god.

8. Roman emperors often communicated with the Senate by letter. It's not impossible

that Seneca got hold of a copy of an authentic letter from Augustus, but it's more likely that he made up the quote that follows.

9. That is, for retirement.

10. The reference is the civil wars in which Augustus (then named Octavian) fought first the killers of Julius Caesar (his countrymen), then his fellow triumvirs Lepidus and Marc Antony, and finally Antony, his brother-in-law. The geographic catalogue that follows traces the course of those civil wars.

11. The men named here were accused of various conspiracies against Augustus during the first decade of his reign (29–19 BC). The Lepidus referred to is not the triumvir but his son.

12. Augustus's daughter Julia scandalized Rome with lascivious behavior and was exiled in 2 BC. The name Iullus, if correct

(it has been supplied by emendation of the text), refers to a son of Marc Antony who was executed for adultery with Julia. Thus, Seneca calls him "an Antony" and implicitly compares Julia to Cleopatra, implying that the liaison of Iullus and Julia created grave danger for Rome.

13. Cicero was consul in 63 BC and had to deal with an attempted coup by Catiline; as a lawyer, two years later, he prosecuted another political troublemaker, Clodius Pulcher; and in the ensuing years, he navigated a perilous path under the First Triumvirate, consisting of Pompey, Crassus, and Julius Caesar.

14. Gnaeus Pompey, the son of Pompey the Great, took up the war against Julius Caesar after his father's death in 48 BC. Many surviving letters from Cicero to Atticus, his longtime confidant, express the kind of

complaint voiced here, but the precise words Seneca quotes are not among them.

15. A figure active in Roman politics in the 90s BC, assassinated near the end of that decade. Seneca is alone in suggesting he might have committed suicide.

16. Like the Gracchi brothers before him, Drusus proposed measures that would have redistributed land to Rome's poorer classes.

17. Seneca here drops the fiction that he's addressing his father-in-law, Paulinus, in a private communication and speaks as one seeking to educate a large readership.

18. That is, as opposed to those who passively indulge their appetites, those who sin in active endeavors at least have the virtue of vigor on their side.

19. "Living" of course means life in the fullest sense, devoted to the "good mind."

20. See note 5 above.

21. The old woman mentioned apparently was wealthy, and, lacking in next of kin ("worn out from burying heirs"), attracts to herself the *captatores*, or legacy hunters, who tried to get such intestate rich to adopt them. The same problem afflicts the man in the next example, who presumably feigns illness because he enjoys the captatores' attentions.

22. The "rods" are the *fasces*, a bundle of rods around an axe, carried before Roman officials to signify their power to impose corporal punishment.

23. Seneca's language here recurs to the analogy between money and time, found often in this essay.

24. This is somewhat contradicted by Seneca's later statement (see chapter 15 below) that the wise are able to anticipate the future.

25. The lines are from Vergil's *Georgics* (3.66–67), where they refer to the need for the cattle farmer not to delay in putting his bulls to the cows, lest illness or old age prevent them from breeding.

26. Papirius Fabianus, who lived during the time of Augustus, was a Roman philosopher whose writings were studied by Seneca in his youth.

27. Another metaphor comparing time to money, in this case to invested capital.

28. Guard dogs were let out at night in Roman streets, but Seneca's image of dogs chasing overzealous lawyers out of court is hyperbolic.

29. The scenario is again that of clientela. The patron is crushed by "his own crowd"; the client, by that of another.

30. The "praetors' spear" was fixed in the ground at the site of a state-sponsored auction,

where the goods of condemned or executed men might be sold off at discount prices. Seneca casts a cold eye on profiteering off such misfortunes.

31. The wrestling ring was well-known, especially in the Greek world, as a place where older males ogled younger ones and often tried to seduce them. Seneca clearly disapproves of the pederastic male relationships more widely accepted in Greece than in Rome.

32. Oil was applied to the skin by wrestlers, to make it harder for their opponents to grip them.

33. Throughout his writings, Seneca uses demonstrative pronouns such as "these" and "those" as though he and his readers were jointly surveying a gallery of human types.

34. The Latin word *exoletus* refers to male prostitutes who were passive sexual partners for other males. Seneca imagines such

youths being employed as servers at dinner parties and for the benefit of randy guests.

35. The Latin term *glabri* refers to slaves whose beard hairs have been shaved or plucked to maintain their boyish, and therefore sexually alluring, appearance.

36. In a Roman context, "mimes" were performers in low-comic skits that imitated daily life, often in its more vulgar or scurrilous aspects.

37. Seneca's examples here of useless scholarship are embarrassing to classicists who still pursue these questions today. Consensus has it that the *Odyssey* was later than the *Iliad*, but there's no agreement on whether the two poems were shaped by the same hand.

38. Seneca goes on in the next few paragraphs to cite a long list of obscure historical questions that he finds useless, or nearly so. It would be contrary to his purpose, and out

of keeping with this series, to footnote these paragraphs in such a way as to explain their allusions. Seneca's point is moral, not historical, as seen in his fervent digression on the fate of Pompey the Great (which *is* annotated). He also seems to enjoy showing off his own knowledge of Roman historical trivia, even while dismissing such facts as a waste of time.

39. Defeated by Julius Caesar at Philippi, Pompey fled to Egypt, where he thought he had an ally in Ptolemy XII, but that ruler sided with Caesar and had Pompey assassinated on his arrival. The "lowest henchman" probably refers to the man who carried out the killing, a former soldier in Pompey's army.

40. See note 26.

41. Seneca says "wisdom," not "philosophy," but the examples he gives below makes clear what sort of wisdom he is thinking of.

42. Seneca skims briefly over the major philosophic schools of his day, beginning with Socrates in the fifth century BC, who preceded the schools but was considered the founder of nearly all. Carneades headed the Platonic Academy during part of its so-called skeptical phase, when all certainty and knowledge were cast into doubt. Epicurus, teaching at Athens in the late fourth century BC, preached the virtues of withdrawal and tranquility. The Stoics, whose teachings Seneca followed most closely, urged the suppression of emotions ("human nature") in favor of reason (as illustrated in another volume in this series, *How to Keep Your Cool*). The Cynics, whose ascetic lifestyle Seneca sometimes claimed to admire, rejected all social convention and hence are here said to surpass human nature.

43. The scenario is once again that of the clientela.

44. The reference is to the assistant who, in many wealthy households, discreetly ("with lips that barely move") reminded the patron of the names of his clients; Seneca's point is that the uncaring, hung over patron in this caricature has had to be told the name of his client over and over again.

45. For Seneca, the greatest goal of moral philosophy was preparation for death (as explored in my previous volume in this series, *How to Die*).

46. The reference to dangerous friendships and conversations attests to the repression of dissidents in Seneca's Rome. Those who associated with men under suspicion could themselves be exiled or arrested.

47. The Latin pun employed here, by which "goods" (*bona*) has both a material and

moral sense, can only be partly captured in English.

48. In his moral writings, Seneca often addresses an imaginary objector or skeptic, as he does here, or even gives that person a voice. For this reason his essays were referred to by early editors as "dialogues."

49. In the mythic tradition, Jupiter was said to have made the night twice as long in order to sleep with Alcmena, mother of Hercules.

50. The story, concerning King Xerxes of Persia, is taken from the Greek historian Herodotus. The invasion force Xerxes led into Greece was so vast it could only be counted by moving small groups, one by one, into an enclosure that held a fixed number of soldiers. Xerxes then wept, Herodotus claimed, at the thought that not one of the host would still be alive a century

later. After the invasion failed, many of these troops lost their lives.

51. Three examples from Republican Roman history. Gaius Marius won fame in Rome's wars but was then elected consul seven times between 107 and 86 BC. Lucius Cincinnatus, famous for having renounced the office of dictator and returned to his plow (in the fifth century BC), was subsequently appointed to a second dictatorship. Scipio Africanus's victory over the Carthaginian general Hannibal (202 BC) prompted some to propose that his statue be placed on the Capitoline, beside a famous image of Jupiter, but Scipio quashed the idea, not wanting to receive the same honors as a god.

52. Referring again to Scipio. Long after his defeat of Hannibal, Scipio's enemies accused him of taking bribes and made several

attempts to put him on trial. Scipio withdrew to his country estate on the coast of Campania, not an "exile," as Seneca terms it, but a rejection of political life.

53. Paulinus was likely in his sixties at the time this dialogue was written.

54. Paulinus was appointed praefectus annonae probably in AD 48, so he might have been in office for seven years before his dismissal in 55. But he had held other public posts before that.

55. Since the grain stocks that Paulinus oversaw were imported from many places (largely from Egypt), Seneca describes him, with typical hyperbole, as keeping the books of the entire globe.

56. Seneca had been a senator through the reign of Caligula and ever afterward took revenge in his writings for the abuses he and his colleagues had suffered. Here he

imagines that the ghost of Caligula, after his assassination (some ten or fifteen years prior), was dismayed to learn that he had left the Romans with even a meager food supply.

57. According to sources, in AD 39 Caligula had a three-mile-long pontoon bridge built across the Bay of Naples simply so that he could ride across it in triumph. He thus imitated Xerxes's crossing the Hellespont (the "arrogant king" of the next sentence). Seneca here implies that the misuse of boats and resources to build the bridge helped cause the subsequent famine, even though the two events were two years apart.

58. Seneca's colorful phrase literally means "while your blood is warm."

59. Seneca returns yet again to the clientela system, in which the client attends the patron as the latter is waking or walking from place to place.

60. That is, a man who's held many high offices, wearing the purple-striped toga that signified his authority.

61. Since Romans had no numbered years as we do, each year was designated by the name of a consul whose term began then. To have the year thus bear one's name was deemed a high honor in Rome.

62. Turannius was the first to hold the office of praefectus annonae, the post later held by Seneca's addressee Paulinus.

63. Seneca uses the term loosely, or even inaccurately, to refer to Turannius's office. By the time of Caligula, Turannius had held the post of praefectus annonae for more than twenty-five years.

64. The funerals of Roman children were held at night and lit by torches. Seneca's point is that since these preoccupied people have spent so little time *living*, they're actually very young.

65. As he often did in "On the Shortness of Life," Seneca here speaks of time in language more commonly used of money.

66. Seneca here gives a rough Latin translation of a Greek aphorism found in Hesiod's didactic poem *Works and Days* (line 369).

67. Sotion was a follower of Pythagorean thought, who briefly converted Seneca to vegetarianism. In another of the *Moral Epistles* (108) Seneca quotes an impassioned speech by Sotion on this subject.

68. Seneca here echoes the attack he made on useless quibbling in chapter 13 of "On the Shortness of Life."

69. Seneca often uses warfare as a metaphor for the struggles of moral endeavor or of life generally. In his treatise *On Benefits*, composed at about the same time as the *Moral Epistles*, he compares human existence to the travails of a city being taken by storm in a siege.

70. The quote is from Vergil's *Aeneid* (8.385–86). The goddess Venus speaks these lines to her husband Hephaestus, on Mount Olympus, referring to the war taking place below between the Italian peoples and the Trojans led by Aeneas.